AFFAIRS:
EMERGENCY TACTICS

Private coaching concerning an affair
Carol Rhodes, Ph.D. CLR@speedlink.net
(248) 651 8282
Norman S. Goldner, Ph.D.
Norgol@earthlink.net
or (248) 299 7989

ALSO BY CAROL RHODES

Why Women & Men Don't' Get Along
(Co-Author, Norman Goldner)

AFFAIRS:
EMERGENCY TACTICS

FROM DISCOVERY TO RECOVERY

CAROL RHODES, PH.D.
With Norman S. Goldner, Ph.D.

SOMERSET PUBLISHING

Copyright @ 1999 by Carol L. Rhodes, Ph.D.

All rights reserved, including the right to reproduce this work in any form whatsoever, without permission in writing from the author, except for brief passages in connection with a review.

Printed in the United States of America

Publisher's Cataloging-in-Publication
Rhodes, Carol L.
Affairs: Emergency tactics: from discovery to recovery/Carol Rhodes.—1st ed.
    5. cm.
    Includes bibliography references.
    Preassigned LCCN: 98-90185

    ISBN 0-9632309-7-2
1. Adultery. 2. Marriage. I. Title
    HQ806.R6 1998   306.73'6
                         QB198-825

Cover Design: C.O. & Co.

For information write to:
Somerset Publishing
P.O. Box 82116
Rochester, MI 48308-2487
Or call: (248) 651-8282
Email: CLR@speedlink.net. If you are unable to obtain this book from your local bookseller you may order it directly from the author. Send $14 + $2.50 for shipping and handling to Carol Rhodes, Ph.D., 71 Walnut, Ste. 109, Rochester, MI 48307.

To my mother Caroline, my brother Richard, and my sister Sandra.

To my children, Rob, Colleen and Bill and to my other children, Seth, Sasha and Aaron.

Most of all to my husband, Norman, for his love, day-by-day encouragement, advice, editorial comments, suggestions, and insistence on equal time for recreation.

ACKNOWLEDGMENTS

My clients have opened their hearts and souls to me in therapy and had confidence that their self-disclosure would be rewarded. They have taught me to appreciate the power of the human spirit in the face of chaos and fear. My reward has been my own growth and development.

I give special thanks to my neighbor and editor, Carole Jonson, whose skill and patience have been of immeasurable help to me. I also want to thank Annabelle McIlnay and Sandra Palmer for their careful editing and assistance with the manuscript.

Contents

Introduction: Discovery to Recovery   8

Section One   What to do When An Affair Is Revealed or Suspected   11
Chapter 1: Affair Anguish   12
Chapter 2: Do's & Don'ts: Managing Affair Facts   25
Chapter 3: Uncovering Deception   41
Chapter 4: Overcoming Inner Chaos   65

Section Two   Categories of Affairs   80

Chapter 5: Affair Types: The Bridge   81
Chapter 6: Self-serving Affairs   96
Chapter 7: Working Through a Repair Affair   109

Section Three   Recreating Yourself   126

Chapter 8: Leaving the Past and Entering the Future   127
Chapter 9: Success Through Separation Or Divorce   145
Chapter 10: Bittersweet   173

Bibliography   175

INTRODUCTION

Case Studies are based upon real people with altered names and circumstances.

AFFAIR DISCOVERY AND RECOVERY

Your partner's affair is not the end of the world. You will not only survive, you will thrive—if you keep your wits about you. What you must do, take charge, is what you're least likely to do. As a psychologist and marriage counselor I've counseled hundreds of couples consumed by the trauma of an affair. I know that you have more power and control than you realize.

Discovering your loved one's affair crushes your ego, brings abandonment fears to consciousness; life becomes a living hell. It turns out you've been living a horrible lie, and now your way of life is in jeopardy. After the initial shock of knowing your mate has deceived you and prefers someone else, there will be an overpowering urge to do something about your pain. If that something is based on emotion rather than reason, you're likely to seriously regret your actions and words.

I want to impress upon you that no matter how much I empathize with your pain or how well I understand your need to rant, scream, rave, and punch (sometimes even to stab and shoot), **I STRONGLY RECOMMEND AGAINST IMPULSIVE ACTION.**

Introduction

Clear thinking disappears when you suspect or discover the person you love and trust is having an affair.

Just when you need an astute, judicious plan of action, the shock turns your rational mind to emotional mush.

When you discover that your mate is unfaithful, what you do or don't do next may heavily affect all following events, for better or for worse! I've learned that mistakes you make at the time of affair discovery may destroy your chances for a reconciliation. Or these initial errors may ruin your chances for a reasonable divorce settlement along with optimum access to your children.

In short, each time you take or fail to take proper action, the positive or negative effects can resonate indefinitely into your future. Wise decisions help your recovery; poor choices may permanently handicap you.

Equally important is understanding what has motivated the affair. There are different causes for affairs:

1. Efforts by the perpetrator to correct a problem in the relationship
2. A signal that the relationship is permanently over
3. A character defect drives the affair

In these two latter instances, there is nothing to do but cut your losses and set yourself up as best you can for the future.

While an affair constitutes the most devastating event for a relationship--short of death--there are two positive possibilities. Reconciliation can lead to a significantly stronger relationship; or, the fatal weakness in the marriage can be dealt with so that everyone's losses are reduced.

It is my philosophy that it's never over until it's over and then it isn't over. Even though an affair may feel like it's the end of your dignity and life, there is much left to be negotiated, even corrected.

There are steps that you can take to make the best of your situation. Consider the recommendations outlined in the book carefully. Then ask yourself, "If I follow these suggestions, will I and my family be better or worse off than if I make other choices?"

Quiet yourself; let your fears go. I have a plan for you which will ease your fears, change your thoughts and provide a plan for action.

SECTION ONE

WHAT TO DO WHEN AN AFFAIR IS REVEALED OR SUSPECTED

CHAPTER ONE

THE ANGUISH OF AFFAIRS

When you have discovered your partner is having an affair or have reason to believe one is in progress, what you do next may determine the course of your life, for better or for worse. If you carefully read this book you will understand everything you need to know about handling the affair and managing yourself during this crisis.

Reactions to affairs vary. Either you feel immobilized or propelled into action--and feelings are never permanent, they slip and slide. Nevertheless, you can manage yourself and make wise decisions.

This chapter describes individuals who reacted to affairs wisely, impulsively, foolishly, or appropriately. They felt driven by circumstances; you have choices.

Adulterers do not usually give their partners affair information; secrets and denial characterize their existence. In the meantime their suspicious mates are filled with anticipatory anxiety and fear.

Sarah and Matt were the exception. Sarah was too busy with children, home and work to attend to changes in her husband, Matt. And, although affair revelation is rare, Matt confessed: He was in the midst of an affair.

Sarah and Len

On the phone Sarah's voice quivered as she told me she had never talked to a psychologist before. What's more, she had never had serious problems. This was an emergency. Her husband, Matt, had left home and she needed help "right now."

In my office for her first therapy session, Sarah, a 38-year-old journalist, sounded very different than she looked. Her clothes were rumpled and mismatched and though she'd evidently made some attempt to control naturally curly hair, curls darted here and there. In contrast, Sarah's voice was low and commanding as she chronologically presented her trauma.

She settled into the couch and pulled a notebook out of her purse. Glancing at the book she said, "To stay calm, I write."

"I'll start at the beginning."

I was leaning against the counter sipping one last cup of coffee, checking my schedule for the day and chatting with my husband Matt.

Out of the blue he said, 'I hate to hurt you but I've got to get something off my chest.

'I'm not sure how to tell you...Jeannie and I are in love and we've decided we're going to be together.

'I'm sorry.'

My cup tipped and coffee splashed as I stared at Matt. He stumbled on. 'We didn't plan this, one thing just led to another.'

Scrambling to make sense of what I'd just heard, I asked, "Are you crazy? What are you talking about?"

I was in shock. I had to hang onto the counter and I thought, I'm having a heart attack.

Jeannie is a friend of mine as well as Matt's police partner. I just couldn't grasp what he was saying. Actually, I was so out of control I thought the next step for me was the emergency room.

Still, I've had enough crisis experience as a reporter that I was able to pull myself together and tell him, 'I need more information. I want to talk to Jeannie right now.'

Matt balked but, I think because he was feeling guilty, he went to the phone. He and Jeannie had a brief conversation that I couldn't make out and then he handed me the phone, 'Here, Jeannie's on the line.'

Matt charged into the family room and picked up the extension. As crazed as I was, I think talking to Jeannie changed everything.

I questioned her: questioned their history together, the possibility of happiness in the face of five children in divorce court, and the huge financial burden Matt would face.

Sarah paused to take a breath. First Jeannie declared her love for Len by telling me she was getting a divorce, but as I piled one threat onto another, she began to fumble with words. She asked me not to do anything hasty and asked to speak to Matt again.

As they spoke, Matt turned ashen and argued with her. Evidently, Jeannie hung up on him.

Sarah didn't stop there. She got Jeannie's husband's work number and began a series of daily calls. She hired a detective to follow Matt. She took pictures of Jeannie going in and out of work. She joined a support group for affair victims on the Internet with other affair victims. She told the kids and her parents. In general, she acted as if she were exposing a political cover-up.

Matt begged Sarah to stop her relentless push to tell the world, but Sarah was in such a crazed state she felt propelled forward. She didn't give up until Matt moved out, refused to speak to her and began a divorce action.

In short, Sarah went from shock to overkill. Had Sarah let things jell she might have avoided the fall-out from her expose`. She, rather than Matt, might have determined the future of the relationship.

What **do** you do when an affair sucks you into an emotional tailspin?

1. The first thing to do is **NOTHING**. The more you want to confront your mate, tell his or her employer, inform family and friends about the betrayal, the more controlled you need to be.

2. Make absolutely sure your mate is actually having an affair. One of the least effective ways of doing this is to confront the alleged offender or his or her alleged lover. You need proof. Going to the source and asking your mate, "Are you having an affair?" is more likely to generate a cover-up than a confession.

3. Control your emotions. Managing the trauma while intellectually processing information is a monumental task. However, it **can** be done.

4. Determine what kind of affair your spouse is involved in. Is your mate a philanderer, someone who takes pleasure wherever it is to be found? Is your beloved involved in a deep emotional relationship with the other party and preparing to leave you? Is the affair situational--

a casual coupling that is unlikely to be repeated? Perhaps your partner arranged for you to discover the affair in order to bring more important matters to the table.

5. Choose expert allies experienced in marital and relationship problems. Once you've chosen this ally (e.g. an attorney and a therapist) consult with them before taking action.

As an illustration of what can happen when you react impulsively, consider the case of Tom and Ally.

Ally and Tom
I answered the phone. Muffled sobs, snaffled words, nose blowing, then, "Can I make an appointment? My husband's left me." I could barely understand her voice on the phone.

After a brief conversation I understood Ally to say that her faithful, loving, family-oriented Tom disappeared into an affair after twenty-three years of marriage. We arranged an emergency meeting. Ally, anxious for pain relief, arrived a half-hour early for her first scheduled therapy session. When she entered the consulting room she slumped into the couch, sobbing.

Without acknowledging me, she blurted, "My husband left yesterday. That's all. He just left. Why did he leave? I can't understand it. He said he was moving out. I thought he meant he was planning a business trip. No! He meant he was leaving us." Sally punctuated each sentence by pounding her fist on her thigh.

Ally, at 41, was a stay-at-home mom, who had just spent her first night without Tom since they married twenty-three years ago.

Crying, choking, wiping her runny nose and eyes, she sobbed, "I don't know what to do. I told him, 'You can't leave me!' He said he was done with the marriage, that he'd been trying to tell me for five years he was unhappy, but I never listened.

"'I'm listening now,' I told him. He wouldn't look at me when he said it was too late! Sobbing louder, Ally slumped further into the couch. "I'll change, I'll change!"

I asked her to tell me something about Tom and their marriage.

"Tom says I wasn't affectionate enough. Well, I don't come from an affectionate family. Can I help that? It's not my nature, but I can change if it's important to him. The trouble is, once he's made up his mind, that's it. He's stubborn. I know he won't be back."

She reached for another tissue, "Then I asked him if there was someone else. He said not, but I think he's lying."

As though one brain cell switched off and another turned on, Ally's hysteria left. She became quiet, limp, still.

In a few moments the composed Ally asked, "What do you think? Do you think he's lying? Do people like him ever return? I want him so much; he's my life. Everything I am has to do with Tom.

"We just came back from a vacation in Colorado and had a wonderful time. He told our friend Jim he was happier now than he had ever been. I don't get it. Tom says one thing and does another.

"Everyone likes Tom, I mean everyone. He always has ideas about what to do and where to go. People are attracted to him. So where am I without him? Nowhere!"

Speaking quietly Ally declared, "I'm a wreck. Tom's all I've got. I depend on him. He's my life. I can't go on without him. I don't mean I'll commit suicide, but I feel like it. I've always loved my house, but now I can't stand being in it alone."

By the end of the session Ally was emotionally exhausted. We agreed to meet in three days. I cautioned her to take no action until we formulated a plan that would be in everyone's best interests.

When we met again Ally was more crazed than before. She had discovered Tom did have another woman and knew many of the details of his affair. Now anger spiced her injury. Quivering with fury, she declared, "I told my family last night. They said to divorce him. This morning I called the boss's wife. Tom's company is very family-oriented. I think she'll talk to her husband, and he'll talk some sense into Tom."

Avoid these Mistakes when Reacting to an Affair

Ally is in "betrayal shock." Like an accident victim, she wasn't able to decipher what happened to her or how to respond. By contacting Tom's employer she set events in motion that will take on a life of their own. If Tom's employer was as family-oriented as Ally believed, her husband's career was now in jeopardy, adding to the problems she already had.

It turned out that the boss's wife did mention Tom's affair to her husband. Tom was called in for a conference and told that his future employment rested on giving up his romance and returning to his family.

Was this a victory for Ally? She wanted the boss on "her side." (One should be very careful what one wishes for; it might come true.) But would the boss's ultimatum make Tom love Ally and not care about the other woman? Even if he did give up his paramour, it's possible Tom would be terminated or no longer be a candidate for promotion.

Actually, Ally's desperate behavior worsened an already devastating situation. Her maneuvers neither put an end to the affair nor remedied the underlying problems in her marriage. Though we can easily understand what she was trying to accomplish and how normal it was to strike out against the person causing so much pain, her actions boomeranged.

Where Ally's action boomeranged, Jeff's action was beneficial and provides an example of a better way to handle an affair.

Jeff and Katie

Katie, 31, and Jeff, 32, had lived together for four years. They were engaged and planned to marry when they were able to buy a home.

Jeff said he had begun to feel uneasy several months ago because as their nest egg grew, Katie's interest in looking at houses diminished. At the same time her good friend, Josh, spent more and more time at their apartment. Jeff liked Josh but told Katie it was inappropriate for her male friend to be camping out with them. Katie indignantly said she had a right to spend time with a friend.

Jeff's unease turned to trauma when he came home from work one Monday night to find Katie and her things had disappeared from their

apartment. There was no call, no "I love you, but this isn't working."

Protecting Yourself Intuitively

Jeff felt as if he'd been run over by a truck. Shocked, body in slow motion, emotions out of control, he was too anxious to eat or sleep. During his sleepless hours he allowed himself to focus on the possibility of an affair between Josh and Katie, an idea he tried to shake out of his mind before Katie left. Now he realized affair clues had been blatant. However, because he didn't want to recognize the truth, he chose to overlook the obvious.

Jeff's other focus that same night became money, the symbol of the togetherness he and Katie shared. Jeff determined to shift their joint account to his name the next morning, terrified Katie had already depleted their savings.

Abandoned, fearful, rage-filled, humiliated, Jeff knew how upset Katie would be when she discovered the empty account. He wavered, fearful of displeasing Katie, momentarily forgetting his devastation. At the same time, he prayed she hadn't beaten him to the bank.

Jeff was getting Katie where he knew it would hurt, and he was also taking what little control he could. After all, he reasoned, he could give Katie her half of the money later. Jeff's desire for the relationship momentarily overwhelmed his intuitive inner alarm system.

Jeff decided he was too emotionally affected to make a reasonable decision and called his father to discuss the situation. His father, who was very fond of Katie, was surprised at this turn of events but agreed, no harm would come from taking charge of the bank account.

By protecting himself financially, Jeff acted in his best interest despite his fears. Since bringing Katie back wasn't an option, protecting finances was, Jeff wisely chose to gain some measure of control and power.

Money in your control can always be given back or magnanimously distributed, but once it's gone, you may find yourself relationship-wise and money-foolish.

Slow, Steady Progress

Jeff's move to protect his finances was positive since Katie had shown by her actions talking before acting was not on her agenda and trust would definitely be an issue in the future.

Consider Val and Ted's situation. Their story shows the benefit of curbing impulsive actions when an affair is discovered. Patience was their strength.

Ted and Val

Val is a 55-year-old who works part-time; her husband, Ted, 59, is in the mortgage business. They've been married for 34 years and have a son and a daughter.

Val called to set up a marital counseling appointment for her and Ted although she wasn't sure he'd attend. Ted's reluctant participation in the first sessions ended when he announced to Val that he couldn't continue the charade: He was involved with another woman.

Val continued therapy, but Ted saw nothing to be gained once he'd used the counseling to "dump" his wife on the therapist.

The usual fireworks followed; Val got angry and told parents, children and friends what Ted had done. Accordingly, everyone chose sides.

Although I cautioned against these impulsive disclosures, Val couldn't contain herself. After the initial damage, she faced the next step: Should she file for divorce or not.

Val spent some agonizing hours deciding whether she wanted to end or maintain the relationship. She finally came down on the side of preserving the marriage--if she could. Moreover, Ted--after his initial bold disclosure that he had a girlfriend--began to waffle. At first he said he'd move out, then decided he might stay. Initially he was sure the marriage was over; later he wondered whether or not he was doing the right thing.

His children applied pressure. His son decided not to invite Ted to his upcoming wedding and his daughter forbade Ted to visit his beloved granddaughter.

Val and I thought this through: If the children cut Ted out of their lives, they could be doing something they would later regret, but their actions might also reduce Ted's ambivalence.

Ambivalence was one of the remaining hopes for Val. If she pushed Ted too far away too fast and too conclusively, she might drive him right into the arms of his lover. True, she could put the hammer to Ted, hoping to bring him to his senses, but the risk seemed too great for an unlikely gain. Val recommitted herself to a long-term strategy of patience and appropriate responses.

Val convinced her son to invite Ted to the wedding. She prevailed upon her daughter to allow Ted to see his granddaughter. Nevertheless, Ted announced he was going to move to an apartment. Val later discovered he'd rented the apartment months prior to his move. But she kept her own counsel and did not make the usual accusations about his lying and deceit.

Val put up with numerous blows to her self-esteem. Ted vacationed with his lady friend at the family cottage. He moved back home for a brief period, then moved out again. Val found love letters Ted and the other woman exchanged. Therapy sessions allowed her to diffuse her understandable pain and anger.

If this couple was ever to reunite it would be because of Ted's inability to act decisively-- a fact that was most difficult for Val to comprehend and accept. I explained, "sometimes near is far and far is near." If Val continued to try to keep Ted and his friend apart, especially since the friend lived in a distant city, the romance might be enhanced. Also, Ted and his lover might not have a chance to know if they were as well suited to one another as they might imagine. Val decided to encourage the relationship to the extent she could. Ted wanted to have his cake and eat it too: He confided in Val when he was miserable.

Rita, Ted's lover, also suffered from Ted's ambivalence, and constantly pressured him to divorce. Eventually she began to issue ultimatums: Either Ted got a divorce or Rita ended the relationship.

This dance of ambivalence, pressure and patience went on for two years when Ted and Rita scheduled a whole summer together. Six weeks into their cohabitation, with Rita constantly stepping up the pressure, Ted became so miserable he couldn't wait for Rita to leave for a new job.

He sheepishly returned to Val, asking to resume the marriage. Val understood he was still ambivalent and would probably remain so. But she preferred the marriage, even if it didn't seem acceptable to other people. Val never stopped believing Ted was basically a good man. Now she was going to get the second chance for which she'd worked so hard.

As you can see, the victim of an affair can influence the consequences and outcomes of this kind of betrayal. Not many people are as patient as Val nor as forgiving. Read on to learn what to do when you discover an affair.

CHAPTER TWO

AFFAIRS IN PROGRESS

DO'S and DON'TS

This chapter specifies the steps to take if your spouse is having an affair. I focus on "emergency measures"--things to do and not to do—to promote the best outcome for you and your family.

DEFINITIONS

First, let's agree on terminology to make sure that we are focusing on the same issues.

Trust is based on a firm belief or confidence in the honesty, integrity, reliability, and correct behavior of another person.

An affair is a secret, ongoing emotional attachment, usually including sexual activity, with a person other than the avowed exclusive partner. Webster's Dictionary defines betrayal as: "To break faith with; to fail to meet the hopes of; to deceive; to be false or disloyal to." Betrayal includes violating the exclusivity clause in the primary relationship by having sex or a significant emotional attachment with another person.

Blaming Yourself

There's special danger to your ego when the relationship is betrayed. Because of your own shortcomings you blame yourself for not being able to hold the other person's interest. Is it possible that some of your attitudes and behaviors "encouraged" the betrayal? Bear in mind it was the other person's decision to violate the relationship. No matter what rationalizations are served up to defend adultery, the person who made the decision to deceive is the responsible party.

After the shock of knowing your loved one has deceived you, there will be an overpowering urge to do something about your pain. If that something is based on emotion rather than reason, you're likely to regret your actions and words.

You Should Proceed Cautiously

Take the needed steps to improve your situation. Read the recommendations below carefully, ask yourself: "If I follow the steps suggested, am I likely to come to more or less harm than if I do it my (impulsive) way?

STEP ONE: Stop!

If you are the victim of an affair, don't take action until you have decided what is in your best interest. Stress, certain to be your companion, should not be allowed to become your master. Stress impairs judgment, inflames passions, crushes the soul, undermines self-esteem, threatens the future and sickens the body.

A betrayal blows one's whole world to smithereens. Since trust is founded on your partner's integrity, ability and character, your initial reactions to a cheating partner include:

- Shock
- Hurt
- Anger
- Dismay
- Emotional vertigo
- Impaired thought processes
- A powerful urge for revenge
- Pessimism
- Rage
- Self-pity
- Low self-esteem
- Guilt
- "Loss of face"
- Humiliation
- The wish to die and/or the wish to kill
- Fear for your lifestyle
- Worry about what will happen to your children
- Retaliation so that the other person experiences your pain
- An overwhelming urge to act to protect your interests
- Appetite loss, sleep problems and heart palpitations

Why do I strongly caution you not to act spontaneously? This is such an important issue I will repeat and amplify the message: Urgency, fear, confusion and other negative feelings take over when you learn your partner is involved in an affair. Your judgment and decision making powers are at low ebb.

"But," you protest, "Am I not entitled to my feelings? Shouldn't I be true to myself?" No. Now is the time to be cautious and deliberate in your calculations and behaviors--if you want the best possible outcome.

Your first task on the road to self-management is to decide carefully when, how, and what to do.

Whatever actions you take, or fail to take, will resonate in your life for years to come, perhaps forever. Therefore, you must determine your goals. What do you want your future to be like?

STEP TWO: Identify and Set Your Goal(s)

Do you want to salvage the marriage or end it? All affairs are trust betrayals, but there are varieties of affairs (discussed later). Keep in mind not all people who betray or who are betrayed wish to end their relationships.

You may change your mind after saying and doing hateful, spiteful or destructive things--however understandable they are--but your spouse may never forget them. To achieve the best outcome, you must have a clear goal. Without a clear goal you can't decide which action to take.

Don't do things which will cut off future alternatives. Don't make a hasty decision and don't assume because you feel strongly about saving or ending the relationship that you won't change your mind. Act in ways which leave your options open but preserve your basic interests. For example, if you need to stop your partner from disposing of marital assets, file the necessary action promptly. But, explain you are doing this to protect your interests, not to hurt the other person.

If you want to preserve the relationship you will take one set of actions. If you want to end the relationship, or if the other party is going to end it no matter what you do, other actions will be in order. What you do or don't do makes a difference.

Affairs in Progress

It's one thing to set goals early on, but you may be so emotionally volatile and confused that making good decisions about the future is beyond you. At this time rely on outside advice to help you formulate your plans. Plans can always be changed later.

You will inevitably walk one of two broad paths: toward reconciliation or toward a divorce. Sometimes you start on one path and switch to the other but usually your earliest decisions determine whether or not you can switch paths. For example, vicious verbal or physical assaults may reveal a side of you the other person will use as further proof the relationship is hopeless.

In one case, the wife became virtually psychotic upon learning there was another woman in the picture. She screamed, demeaned her husband in front of others including friends, relatives and the children, threw things at him and showed such a violent primitive side of her personality that her husband resolved to never even attempt to resume the marriage. Although she later apologized for her behavior, he could not get her rage out of his mind.

Increase your options; don't burn your bridges. It's never over till it's over--as long as you leave yourself room to maneuver.

This second step, identifying and setting your goals will give you guidelines for the future. It will help you make the best of an already serious problem, instead of turning it into a disaster. You will be taking measures which will improve your chances of having things work out in your best interest.

Before considering Step Three, let me give you some suggestions for what to do and what not to do if an affair is in progress. These will help you lay the groundwork, to achieve the best outcome--given your particular goals--for your specific situation.

Take the Right Steps

Let's assume you have no doubt whatsoever your partner is having an affair. However, if this fact is yet to be established, consult **Chapter Three, Uncovering Deception: A Possible Affair.** Whatever you've done up to this point, or may do next, will be critical to your future. The following DOs and DON'Ts are intended to:

- Give you time to develop necessary information
- Engineer the best possible outcome for you and your loved ones
- Keep you from making inappropriate choices when you are most vulnerable

Being Smart About Your Partner's Affair

What are the long term interests? That depends on you. If you want to keep your options open and maximize your alternatives, before you take action decide:

- Do you want to continue the marriage?
- Do you want to get the best property settlement you can?
- Do you want to promote the best post-marital parenting situation?

Whatever you believe to be in your best interest can be accomplished; first by specifying your goals, then by asking three fundamental questions before you take any action.

Those questions are:

- Will my actions advance my interests?
- Will my actions be neutral to my interests?
- Will my actions negatively impinge on my goals?

STEP THREE: Utilize These DOs and DON'Ts

DO consult a domestic relations, family law attorney
DON'T make threats about taking legal action

Marriage is a legal as well as a social, spiritual, emotional, psychological and financial contract. Unless you are truly exceptional, you did not research the laws that apply to marriage before you wed. Now is the time to find out what laws apply to your circumstances.

If you want to maintain the marriage, you may fear involving an attorney because your partner could take this as an affront and leave you. Or, perhaps your partner has subtly brought the affair to your attention with the hope that you will end the relationship, thereby putting you in the position of breaking up the family.

You may object to a private consultation with an attorney because you disapprove of operating in an underhanded manner. However, in this situation it is unwise to be "an open book." Being open limits your alternatives.

"I don't have the $2,000 to retain counsel or the fee for a consultation," is another common concern. While a family law attorney isn't allowed to take a divorce case on contingency--to do legal work and collect later based upon the settlement--many attorneys offer complimentary initial interviews. Use this interview to discover your rights and obligations. Ask for material to read to help you understand the legal implications of your situation.

Remember, attorneys are counselors as well as litigators. Virtually any lawyer will tell you it is better not to make mistakes than to try to correct them. Therefore, it is in your best interest to consult with someone who understands the law and how it applies to your particular case.

DO keep your own counsel
DON'T confront your partner

Do not make idle, ill-informed threats about what you are going to do to punish or ruin the betrayer. (A betrayer is a person who has pledged to do one thing--be monogamous and loyal--but secretly violates that pledge. If your partner ends the relationship but has not violated your trust, that is unfortunate, but it is not a betrayal.)

If you don't know the law, you may make inflammatory statements you can't back up. For example, most states have "no fault" statutes. It is a hollow threat to state you won't give your mate a divorce, that you will fight a divorce and hold your spouse hostage to the marriage

You cannot deny another person a divorce. No fault statutes specify that either party can file for or receive a divorce for a minimal reason: The objects of matrimony have irreparably broken down.

Focus instead on the issues of spousal and child support, property division, visitation and custody. If there's a possibility of a divorce or separation, you are well advised to keep these latter considerations in the forefront of your decision making.

I am not advocating legal counsel to obtain a divorce. I want you to know your rights.

The following case illustrates the importance of protecting yourself legally. Mary avoided attorneys because she wanted her marriage to continue despite indisputable knowledge that her spouse was untrustworthy.

Mary and Ned

An emotionally and physically battered wife for 43 years, Mary initiated a divorce at the insistence of her children, who knew their father, Ned, had been involved with a lover for years. The court enjoined Ned from disposing of their major assets, much to his displeasure.

Ned seemed to come to his senses, asking Mary to give him another chance and they reunited. Ned's words begging forgiveness and another chance meant nothing, but they did buy him enough time to get his act together.

Once the injunctions were lifted, Ned began to hide assets and move money into secret accounts. He even tried to persuade Mary to "temporarily" remove her name from the house deed so he could barter it for a better and bigger dwelling.

Soon, Mary became aware that Ned was not interested in her and even regarded her with contempt. The children again convinced her to file for divorce. However, by this time Ned had cleaned up, switching and cashing in bonds, money market funds, stocks and savings accounts.

Although everyone urged Mary to protect herself financially for her future, she did not. While Mary did not protect herself monetarily she was brave enough and wise enough with her children's counsel to follow through and divorce a cheating, mean spouse who she thought would "mellow" with time.

DO manage anger and negative feelings
DON'T let powerful emotions overwhelm you

At our best levels of functioning, we are more rational than we are emotional and habitual. When we are stressed and face threats to our basic security, our rational powers are impaired, our primitive emotional, physiological systems take over. In this state, we are in the greatest danger of working against our own interests.

When chased by a tiger you need a shot of adrenaline to help you up a tree. However, when you are faced with the complications involved in an affair, adrenalizing yourself only gets you into trouble.

Do not give in to your emotions under stress. Now is the time to exercise self-control. Before you take any action weigh the effects of what you plan to do, with future considerations in mind.

I strongly recommend you talk your feelings through with a wise friend or a therapist experienced in crisis counseling. Give serious consideration to their recommendations before you do or say anything.

It is also a good idea to consult a family law attorney to find out what legal implications accompany your actions or failure to act appropriately. In future chapters I will discuss attorney recommendations.

This is your relationship, so be smart, control your emotions and use your head. In other words, proceed with caution though your brain is filled with the urge to question, demand, cry, scream, yell and argue.

Also, refrain from informing the world about your situation.

DO think before talking
DON'T tell the children

The betrayer has damaged you and the children, why not tell them what kind of a lousy person and parent h/she really is? It is natural to want allies, to shame the person who has betrayed you.

However, consider whether or not it is in the children's best interests to be told about the affair. Remember, you are deepest in your pain and shallowest in your judgment. Whether or not you and your spouse decide to reconcile, aligning the children against the other parent will increase your problems and theirs. Don't tell the children about your spouse's affair out of anger and revenge.

DO curtail your actions
DON'T follow your impulses

If you do the first thing that comes to mind, you're likely to place it first on your "List of Regrets." Your intuition and impulses may be O.K. to follow in non-critical matters but responding to an affair requires thought, patience and planning.

By all means, protect yourself if the situation calls for it. It is necessary to be reactive and spontaneous when you are in immediate danger. Though you feel as if you're in danger, in truth you are not. Therefore, impulsive reactions to protect yourself aren't required when you discover an affair.

DO maintain your integrity
DON'T try to please the perpetrator

Throwing yourself at your mate's mercy, begging her/him to give up the other party and stay with you, may give you some temporary gain, but is ineffective in the long run. Inducing guilt and pity provides only short-lived gratification. Your mate will soon revert to previous behavior.

The implications of an affair are so frightening many people react by blaming themselves and trying to please the person having the affair. The underlying motive of trying to please is to win the other person back. Don't follow this path. Providing your partner with more sex than s/he ever dreamed of will not do the trick either. This is a transparent tactic and the likely result is that you wind up feeling more, rather than less rejected.

DO have patience
DON'T expose the affair unless it is to your advantage

It is a relief to share our burden, gain sympathy and perhaps assistance. Sharing your pain and plight with others is a holdover from childhood, when we go to our parents and other authorities to put things in order. The betrayed party often calls upon relatives, friends, or the employer of the betrayer to persuade their mate to abandon an affair.

However natural it is to seek sympathy and allies, it's the wrong thing to do unless you've carefully thought it through.

Once you make others, such as your parents, aware of the affair you may close off possibilities of reconciliation. The adulterer now knows that significant others know, and may be too embarrassed to take the needed steps toward reconciliation.

DO keep silent
DON'T contact the spouse or significant other of the person involved with your mate

It seems logical: "I'll tell the spouse what's going on and that will put an end to the affair." Nice try. It won't work and it will cause even more problems.

Wouldn't the revenge be worth it? Wouldn't you be getting back at the person who has encouraged the betrayal? Why should you have to suffer when the perpetrators go their merry way? They should suffer too. However, you'd better be sure this is the best tactic to reach your real goals. Revenge often backfires.

DO act in your best interest
DO'NT call your partner's employer

"I'll call the boss who will talk some sense into my loved one." If the affair is an office romance, you may think the employer will fire the offending party. But, stop and think. It might be your spouse who is fired, or both parties.

Also, consider that your spouse may be quietly labeled for no promotions. Is this in your best interests, even if you get a divorce?

Is an unemployed or under-employed "ex" in a position to continue to support you and/or your children?

DO take charge of circular thinking
DON'T drive yourself crazy asking "Why?"

The overall picture emerges gradually, but it takes time to play out what was going on historically. Do not ask "Why?" While questions are natural, interpretations differ, and you will understand the situation differently than your spouse.

Your questions will be numerous. You want to know what led up to the affair. You want details about the affair. You hope to determine why the marriage was deficient, if it was. You ask why your spouse found the other person attractive and why you were not. You try to sort through the psychological intricacies of the affair.

All these questions and more come to mind but won't be answered for a long time.

More importantly, you seldom receive the answers you desire. You will discover a number of concrete facts but the emotional, psychological affair details which will satisfy and calm you may never be known.

DO act with dignity
DON'T physically or verbally assault the betrayer

When you've caught the betrayer "red handed" your spouse is likely to be contrite and feel guilty. This is not the time to become verbally or physically abusive. Even though you've been betrayed, attacking intensifies the problems, does not solve them. Specifically, don't physically attack the other party. No matter how justified you feel, the police and courts will not sympathize with you.

DO keep your own counsel
DON'T tell the betrayer everything you know

"Never admit; deny everything," is the credo followed by most people having affairs. Trying to convince the betrayer to stop lying by telling his or her everything you know about his or her activities is a mistake and gives information you will probably regret supplying. It enables your spouse to take counter measures to neutralize the effects of your knowledge.

To summarize, first reactions to the discovery of an affair are sometimes violent or, almost without exception, "stupid." Because stressful situations are accompanied by poor judgment, people often regret their initial responses.

You must Act in your Own Best Interest

The point I want to make in this chapter and throughout the book is: You need direction since you are driven by runaway emotions and can't think clearly. Gradually you will settle down and be able to sort out affair-fact versus affair-fiction. But at this moment in time, taking care of yourself first is critical.

To reiterate:

1. ***Do not*** make threats about taking legal action. Consult a family law attorney.
2. ***Do not*** let your powerful emotions overwhelm you. Manage anger and negative feelings.
3. ***Do not*** tell the children. Think before talking.
4. ***Do not*** follow impulses. Curtail actions.
5. ***Do not*** try to please the perpetrator. Maintain integrity.
6. ***Do not*** expose the affair unless it is to your advantage. Have patience.
7. ***Do not*** contact the spouse or significant other of the person involved in the affair with your mate. Keep silent.
8. ***Do not*** call your mate's employer. Act in your best interests.

9. **Do not** drive yourself crazy asking "Why"? Take charge of circular thinking.

10. **Do not** physically or verbally assault the betrayer. Act with dignity.

11. **Do not** tell the betrayer everything you know. Keep your own counsel.

The next chapter tells you how to determine whether an affair is in progress, how to sort out suspicions and intuition from fact. If your partner isn't forthright (and s/he seldom will be), how do you gather facts and avoid creating serious problems in the process?

CHAPTER THREE

UNCOVERING DECEPTION: A POSSIBLE AFFAIR

Gathering Information: Suspicion or Reality

You sense all is not well in your relationship, what's more, you feel suspicious. Bits of information and fears about an affair intrude and rob you of peace. You wonder and worry. Yet, when you ask your partner, "Is there another person?" the answers are: "Don't be silly. What's wrong with you?"

Alternately afraid you are right, hurt the relationship has reached an impasse, angry your partner has put you in this indecisive position, and ashamed you are entertaining destructive thoughts, you keep questioning yourself. Does the information you have mean what you think it means? Is it true? Is it a lie?

Fears, suspicions and intuitive knowing keep you unsure of your relationship, circumstances and future. That's why concrete information is critical. You need to know if an affair is in process. And, if so, you want to be in the position of making a determination about how to proceed. Otherwise, all the power is in your partner's hands.

Finding Truth
As quickly as you suspect a lie, take action to free your mind by collecting and evaluating the evidence. Without information, you move back and forth, first worrying that

an affair is in progress and wondering what to do about it, then pretending everything is O.K. Neither position is real, and while you're living in dream land, your life as you've known it, is evaporating. Evidence will either put your emotions at rest or put you into a new space in life.

Taking action helps settle and soothe emotional turmoil. This doesn't mean it's easy to take action. It is not because it puts your suspicions into a real form. Remind yourself, what you suspect may not be true.

Gathering Information

At this point you need concrete information regarding the possibility of an affair. You need more than suspicions and intuition. How do you go about obtaining and evaluating evidence? What should you do with your information?

First, develop a fact sheet regarding opposite sex contact, including the information below. Has your spouse had:

> 1. Unexplained breakfast, luncheon, dinner dates, and coffee tête-à-têtes (time, date and place)
>
> 2. Home or motel visits
>
> 3. Written material (cards and letters)
>
> 4. Suspicious telephone calls
>
> 5. Time with someone else walking, talking, sitting in cars

Does this mean an affair is in progress? If you can answer yes to two or more of these items, your spouse is having an inappropriate friendship, if not an affair. It may not be a full blown emotional and sexual affair, but for your peace of mind you need more explanation.

Some situations raise questions which need investigation. Remember, your partner may deliberately mislead you, twist behavior and words, or out and out lie. Sorting lies from reality is tricky, as Rachel's story shows.

Rachel and Jake

Although Rachel was suspicious of her husband's activities, she chose not to dig into the details. Jake, 35, was seldom home. He worked hard to keep his printing business profitable. He had joined a semi-religious, philosophical organization, and began spending weekends and evenings with group members. In fact, he said one of the women was a reincarnation of his dead sister and he "had to delve into her psyche."

Rachel was skeptical but viewed her husband as a brilliant man with unusual ideas. She expected his involvement in the group to pass. Yet, months later Jake was more, rather than less, an active group participant. Rachel felt alienated and angry. She was working full time as a secretary as well as being the primary care taker for their 2-year-old daughter, Melinda.

Pregnancy had been thrilling after praying and waiting for eight years. Because they were so crazy about the baby, Rachel said she found it inconceivable Jake would have an affair.

Though she suspected possible involvement with the "reincarnated" woman, she didn't investigate. Instead, she held on to the card from Jake saying he would always love her, that she was in his heart.

Jake didn't give her this generic card as a personal message, but Rachel took the words literally. They soothed her while she denied what she suspected.

As it turned out, Jake was having an affair and soon began a divorce action. Rachel's denial and failure to act cost her emotionally and financially. She lived through months of fear, anxiety and confusion. Jake surprised and shocked Rachel again when interrogatories were ordered by the court and she discovered he had taken advantage of owning his own business and secreted funds.

If you feel suspicious and uneasy about your relationship, take action. You have nothing to lose and everything to gain.

Focusing on Facts

While gathering information keep in mind the following:

1. Every bit of information will not be available nor will you be able to answer the question, "Why is s/he having an affair?"

2. You should take what your spouse says with a grain of salt; what is said is definitely questionable and may very well be a lie.

3. You should not verbalize any suspicious evidence either to your spouse or to the world.

DO NOT TAKE ANY OF YOUR PARTNER'S WORDS SERIOUSLY.

Fact: A person who tells lies is a liar. A liar's words are not meant to convey information. Rather, their words are meant to confuse and distract.

DO NOT DRIVE YOURSELF CRAZY WITH A NEED FOR EXCESS INFORMATION.

Fact: You will never have all affair information, particularly the emotional information you seek. "Why?" will not be answered now, nor will questions such as, "Do you love this other person?"

DO NOT REPORT DETAILS YOU LEARN OF THE AFFAIR BACK TO YOUR PARTNER.

Fact: Silence is golden. Confide only in your therapist, one trusted friend or your attorney.

These facts are difficult to digest because each opposes normal relationship interaction. Be suspicious if your spouse resents questions regarding his or her whereabouts, suggests you are jealous or "grilling" her/him. Interest in a mate's activities is part and parcel of an intimate connection.

Beware of becoming obsessed by finding out all the details of an affair. Scott's story presents the results of such an obsession. Scott's wife's behavior was blatantly suspicious, and since Scott took time before beginning the information-gathering process, we can guess he feared the reality of betrayal. When Scott did have affair evidence, he kept it to himself. However, once he began the information-gathering process, he couldn't stop obsessively pursuing details.

Scott and Dee

On the phone 52-year-old Scott was affable and light-hearted, sounding cavalier about setting up a counseling appointment. His attorney referred him, he said. As a therapist I know this is a signal the marriage is not only in trouble, it may be over.

In his first therapy session Scott's easy-going phone persona matched his presentation of himself. He owned a gun shop and arrived dressed like a cowboy in boots, plaid shirt and jeans with a big silver buckled belt. To complete the picture he had a wrestler's build with cowlicky hair darting here and there.

Scott appeared to be managing his emotions with difficulty. "O.K. I'm here because my wife, Dee, filed for divorce last month but doesn't want anyone to know. She says she's not sure she wants a divorce, but she needs space. She continually says she needs space.

"I may look like I'm O.K., but I'm crazy as a loon inside. I feel like crying, but of course I don't; I'm a man. I'm suspicious as hell, and I'll tell you why.

"My wife is 43. We've been married forever, it seems. But actually it's only been 23 years. She was 20, I was 29. So, you see, I was an older man. I think I've been like a father to her. Anyway, I digress.

"I'm constantly analyzing the problem, trying to figure out what's going on. When we had been married four years, my wife had a dalliance. I call it that because I'm not sure what it amounted to.

"I found out Dee had been visiting a single man at his apartment in Davidson when I was at work. She'd been taking our baby son with her. When I confronted her, she first denied it. Eventually she confessed when I showed her the card "to a loving friend" I'd discovered.

"Dee said the relationship was nothing; there was no reason to worry. She loved me, she simply needed company. That was pretty hard to believe, but I did.

"I was mad about Dee and wanted to believe it. This time I'm finding it harder to believe she just wants 'space.' I'm up all night plotting, planning and worrying.

"I want therapy because I don't want to do anything stupid if there's a chance to continue our marriage. We have three kids who need her."

He took a deep breath and went on. "The difficulty for me is that she's gone for long periods, she says she's shopping. Dee is a shopper, believe me, but no one can be gone as long as she is and just be shopping.

"She wanted 'space' so she went up north for the weekend with her girl friend. But, she wouldn't leave a phone number or say where she was staying. Doesn't that seem unlike a mother? What if something happened?"

While Scott talked he stared at me, never asking for an opinion, but seemed to check responses, constantly scanning for facial expressions.

"If I ask Dee where she's going or who she's with, she says, 'There you go again stirring everything up, trying to capture me. I need space. I do not like your questioning my every move. What's wrong with you? You're trying to control me.' She turns whatever I say back on me. It makes me crazy."

I assured Scott he wasn't crazy, suspicious behavior arouses fear.

Starting the second session Scott said, "I might as well tell you, I've hired a private detective. As I said last session I don't trust Dee's excuse that she wants 'space.' So far, following her hasn't turned up much. She's gone shopping but then the detective lost her for a couple of hours."

Deciding What to Do

Good, Scott had made a decision to hire a private detective. Since Dee is being mysterious, leaving home for many hours and overnight without informing the family of her whereabouts, she's behaving suspiciously.

Scott's private investigator put a tracking device on Dee's Lexus and gave Scott the printout, basically a map which showed the car traveling down named streets with length of time at every stop.

Dee's whereabouts were no longer secret. She was spending time with another man. Scott was able to confront Dee based on facts.

In spite of Dee's behavior Scott needed and wanted the relationship, and he prayed all would be well. Dee lost interest in the other man and dropped the divorce action. But, Scott's need for information fueled many disagreeable, angry confrontations.

Scott finally gained control. He stopped verbalizing his fears and asking questions regarding his wife's behavior.

Nevertheless, it will take a long time for Scott to trust Dee again--if ever--and feel comfortable with her. However, he said he was willing to put everything he had into establishing a new, better partnership.

Don't Question a Liar

Confrontations based on suspicions and intuition are nonproductive. You need facts. You know you are not going to get answers from your partner, so stop asking. And stop asking questions of yourself.

Gather the information you need to make your own decision about the possibility or reality of an affair. First, accept the fact your loved person may be a liar. Questioning a liar is not only nonproductive and time consuming, in the end, you'll gain nothing but confusion and delay.

Uncovering Lies, Secrets and Deceptions

Why do you feel crazed when you realize the person you love has lied? You've certainly told lies, heard lies: Lies viewed as momentary, little white lies are a part of social living. Who hasn't said "I'm fine" when you're not, or "I like that outfit" when you thought it mediocre or ugly.

You base your life on trust. You accept and trust your spouse when s/he says s/he's at work or loves you or that she's gotten a raise. In other words, you accept, trust and believe the information your spouse gives. When you discover your trust is based on a false premise provided by your partner, you are devastated.

Lies change history. If your partner comes home from a business meeting and you make love, you feel close and intimate. However, if you discover s/he was intimate with another person after the meeting, you feel disgraced and used. What had been love making you view now as animalistic sex. Not love. Deception excludes intimacy. More than that, your whole history together becomes suspect. What else is not as it seemed?

Peace of mind and the ability to assess life depend on trust. When you are told "I grew up on the East Side of Detroit" or, more importantly, "I love you," you trust it is so. You believe. The bedrock of your relationship depends on your belief in each other.

Once suspicious, little bits of information stay in your mind. You don't want them, but they are there. Your mind begins to search for more. "No. It isn't true. I'm making much ado about nothing. It's simply a feeling." Nevertheless, life has to do with trust and tacit knowing. That's why small bits of information are frightening. You feel your partner is distanced, changed and preoccupied. Should you trust your intuition?

You use intuition and perception to understand others. You live in your mind. You read others and determine meaning in glances, body language, talk and feelings. You check out the other for reciprocation. At times you've found yourself doubting people or interpreting behavior and, without verification, believing your thoughts. Consequently, when you detect subtle changes in an intimate relationship you not only question your partner, you question yourself.

Trust isn't everything in a partnership, but without trust there is little else.

Intimate relationship expectations mean you are emotionally and physically safe with and from your partner. In a world where people are indifferent, sometimes hostile, you expect to be cared for and secure at home.

Trust is the cornerstone of the feeling that you are at home, safe and secure. However, when you fear an affair is in progress, you feel anxious and wary and home is no longer a safe sanctuary.

In an untrustworthy relationship, passion suffers; vitality is exhausted; generosity in fact and in spirit disappears; guardedness and suspicion take its place.

Suspecting an affair, you turn in on yourself. You think, "I must be wrong. It can't be true." Still, your heart pounds with fear. You think: "I have a feeling something's wrong, some small difference catches my attention."

At the same time you're relieved, "It can't be true, I'm making something out of nothing:" and for a moment your mind turns away to rest, the feeling is discounted.

When you suspect an affair, should you trust your intuition? Yes, because unless you doubt yourself and your relationships on a daily basis, you have to trust feeling--the feeling that something is wrong.

Collecting Evidence

Collecting evidence means skulking around, being your own private detective or hiring one. Information is critical. Guessing, intuitively knowing or asking may be helpful, but facts are essential. To acquire evidence means acting in ways that are antithetical to individual privacy and may be against your code of ethics. Keep in mind, however, if an affair is in progress, your partner has already violated societal, marital and personal ethics.

When you've exhausted all information avenues available to you, consider the following:

1. Look through wallets or billfolds.

2. Check phone bills for unusual or repetitive numbers.

3. Establish a diary of phone hang-up dates and times.

4. Examine Franklin planners, any daily planners.

5. Keep track of time away from home or unaccountable lunch dates.

6. Track saving and checking for monies withdrawn.

7. Note lessened sexual interest or new sexual techniques.

8. Pay attention and keep written track of a person your partner talks about at length.

9. Tape the home phone (tapes are only for your edification, they cannot be used in court).

10. Tape the car phone (checking to make sure it's legal).

11. Put a voice-activated tape recording machine in his or her car phone (checking to make sure it's legal).

12. Have a tracking device attached to his or her car.

13. When s/he leaves the house for an errand, follow.

Why would you embarrass and humiliate yourself or stoop to such despicable behavior? First, because you must know the state of your relationship for emotional and mental health. Second, because it is imperative you protect your family and finances.

Private detective work is done silently. This bears repeating because you'll have a powerful need to let your partner know you aren't a fool; you have certain evidence and that you have a plan. While collecting evidence **DO NOT** share this information. Keeping silent may seem like an impossibly difficult task, but it is absolutely crucial. You must contain yourself.

If you want the best outcome, it is essential to face facts and be action oriented. Take the case of Kate and Jerry.

Kate and Jerry

The smell of cigarette smoke and perfume proceeded Kate's entrance into the therapy office. At 39, Kate looked 10 years younger. Summer shorts made her legs look like a little girl's, barely shaped and small-boned. Kate's personality was upbeat, enthusiastic and earnest; she smiled happily.

But her cheerleader presentation was deceptive. Sitting on the edge of the chair, she spoke in an intense staccato fashion, "I feel very nervous and jumpy inside. I can hardly sit still. I'm depressed. I can't make myself get out of bed in the morning."

Kate scratched at her arms and hands "My husband has been having an affair. I've suspected it for four months. When I asked him, he denied it. Now I have proof."

Kate explained she has been stalking her husband, Jerry: checking his mileage, tracking his time away from work and asking him directly, "Are you involved with someone else?"

Jerry had an affair six years ago. In therapy Kate said, "I went through hell then, so I knew for sure by his actions and talk he was doing it again. He denied any involvement, and his denial threw me off slightly. I don't know why, because six years ago he denied and lied through his teeth. But this time, I didn't wait, I began to snoop through his 'locked' briefcase.

"Locks don't mean a thing to me. I've learned to break any code. In his briefcase I found love notes in the margin of his graduate school papers. "N, you are beautiful. I've never known anyone like you."

With this discovery, Kate placed a voice-activated tape recorder in Jerry's car. The first night she played it back and found nothing. The next day when she rewound the tape, she heard, "Sweetheart, how was your night?" plus more endearments and intimate talk.

Kate had a tracking device put on his car. When Jerry said he had a meeting, Kate knew exactly where he was and whether the meeting was business or play.

Since Kate had been through this once, we might imagine she would immediately tell Jerry to take a hike, know how to manage herself, determine her plan and proceed. On the contrary, Kate said, "We had a terrible time six years ago and I'm in a worse state now, if that's possible. I can't believe he'd do it again knowing what we went through last time." Kate swallowed, choking on her words, her eyes filled with tears.

With evidence in hand, Kate confronted Jerry, and after two months of wrangling, he confessed. But obviously the problem wasn't solved. Kate immediately set up therapy sessions to figure out why she continued to desire a relationship with a cavalier and uncommitted liar.

Avoiding the Trap of Making Emotion-Clouded Judgments

Kate was smart to spring into action both in obtaining evidence and setting up therapy appointments. Emotions cloud judgment. It is next to impossible to calm and steer oneself expediently and wisely through an emotional trauma. Therapy is essential because the therapist is an objective, trained person who can understand and evaluate issues Kate is unable to recognize.

Protecting Your Short- and Long-term Interests

As soon as you have concrete evidence of an affair, see an attorney and secure your finances.

I strongly suggest you obtain expert legal counsel from a family law attorney who belongs to your state and national sections of the bar associations. There are other experts, such as a certified public accountant and a financial planner, you may want to consult later.

To help you determine if the attorney you've selected is the best one to meet your needs, ask the following questions:

1. Do you specialize in family law?

2. To what family law organizations do you belong?

3. What, if any, positions have you held in those organizations?

4. What is your position about affairs in marriage or committed relationships?

You can also ask for:

- A complementary interview so you and the attorney can each decide if you want to work together.
- Details about attorney fees, what they will cover and when they are due.
- An idea of how quickly you will get responses to your questions and concerns.

An attorney will give you information about your rights given the length of your marriage, number of children, financial assets and debts, and emotional damage incurred by the affair. The attorney will also provide you with general facts regarding how the divorce process works. You are gathering information. Seeing an attorney does not mean you are beginning a divorce process.

Securing Your Finances

Start with this idea. Since you have been deceived personally, it is possible to be deceived in other areas. Do not fear ruffling your partner's feathers by taking money out of savings or putting a stop order on stocks and other assets. It is essential you protect all finances. Marriage is a partnership; in effect, it is a business.

Finances are concrete and should be unemotional, yet you've found it's difficult to make the decision to take action and protect assets. Women, in particular, fear action will upset the violator, so inaction becomes the woman's credo. Men, on the other hand, act aggressively, want to solve the problem **now**.

Fearing your partner will leave if you aren't sweet and loving, you hesitate to secure monies and other assets. You may be the nicest person in the world and give your partner all assets, only to have her/him leave anyway. If you haven't secured your assets, not only will your partner be gone, but so will financial security. It doesn't make sense to take care of your partner's sensibilities, not upset your mate after s/he's broken your heart.

No one else will take care of you; you must take care of yourself. Spouses and lovers involved in affairs say, "You never have to worry. No matter what happens, I'll take care of you." Wrong! They only take care of themselves. They can't help it. They feel sorry and guilty and truly believe they intend to do the right thing.

However, after those initial guilty, sorry feelings diminish, taking care of you seldom happens. Anger, recriminations and feelings for the new person eat into the generous declarations made to you.

You desperately want to believe your spouse's expressed desire to care for you is there and will be put in place, but beware, we tend to believe what we want to believe and disregard facts.

Though you're confused and undetermined as to where the relationship is going, you must secure assets.

Why Have You Been Abandoned?

Interspersed with "Is it true?" and "What should I do?" is "Why?" "Why have I been abandoned?" If you knew why your partner became involved in an affair, you would understand, solve the problem, soothe and unconfuse yourself. You would know what to do about finances, the children and the future. This seldom happens.

When you discover the possibility of infidelity you are thrown into an emotional and situational crisis.

But you are not a leaf in his or her wind. Regardless of your perception of your own weakness, you are powerful. You can discover the truth, handle emotional trauma, grasp the significance of the affair and determine your path with or without the relationship.

True, you will have difficulty thinking clearly and taking action. This is because you are dealing with so many unknowns.

First, sort out what is fact and what is fiction: An affair is in progress. That is fact. Fiction is denying and explaining away affair facts.

Yesterday you trusted your partner. Today trust is an issue. You no longer trust this person.

More importantly, you don't trust yourself, since your spouse, the most important person in your life, is suddenly a stranger--someone other than who and what you believed.

Life as you've known is a sham. You feel disconnected, separated from your relationship core and essentially separated from yourself.

Why is an affair or the possibility of an affair so shattering? An affair is not anticipated; there is no rehearsal. Life management skills don't include: If your spouse has an affair you take steps l, 2 and 3.

The intimacy of a committed relationship precludes affairs. In traditional marriage vows you sign a contract to remain together "until death do us part."

Infidelity breaks the marital contract, violates personal trust and betrays the relationship.

Sorting Out Why People Have Affairs

You fell in love, married or committed to a monogamous relationship, and now your partner is dancing the love dance again with someone else.

You feel jealous because someone else has been chosen. You are jealous because you aren't in his or her altered state, having fun, feeling euphoric and preoccupied. Instead, you are despondent, disturbed and depressed. You feel abandoned.

The experience of both the deceived and the deceiver have to do with mystery, elusiveness and the unknown. The deceiver has high excitement and elevated feelings; the deceived has high anxiety and overwhelming fear.

Minds are caught in the pursuit of the unknown. The deceiver spins an illusion of life's ultimate dream: the perfect relationship. The deceived's mind spins in despair: Is the marital relationship fragmented or totally destroyed?

An affair is romance. Romance is love without the aggravations and irritations of real life. How dare s/he catapult her/himself into another dimension and leave you behind trapped in real life!

If your partner confesses, you may be disconcerted momentarily. In your eagerness to resolve your devastation and anger you may misconstrue the reason for this sudden admission of truth from your partner.

Determining When Confession Is Betrayal

When you suspect an affair you want to know, "Is love involved?" Although this seems a romantic and innocent question for such a complex situation, the question gets to the core of the problem. If love is the answer, you feel your own relationship is over. However, deceivers do not definitively say, "Yes, I love _____."

In fact, plan on denial of any emotional involvement. Your partner will tell you s/he barely knows the other person or, "S/he's just a friend, s/he doesn't mean a thing to me." In fact, if your partner confesses, although the question of love may be first on your mind, what you really need to know is what the confession means.

DO NOT BE STUPID
Even if your partner has confessed or is sorry remember, talk is cheap. **DO NOT BE STUPID**. Affair confession, unless followed by impeccable behavior and marriage counseling, is dangerous and leaves you vulnerable. It leads you to believe all is well and the relationship is back on track.

You have to make sure you stay in the driver's seat. With concrete, irrefutable information, you must make your own decision about how you will proceed.

Once a clandestine sexual relationship exists, the marital contract/commitment is broken. Everything changes. Sex means intimacy; sex equals a shift from an intellectual, platonic, flirtatious friendship to a serious, life changing, threatening situation. You are in danger if your partner admits sexual activity: danger from AIDS and a multitude of other sexually transmitted diseases. So, obtaining information about your partner's activities protects you physically as well as mentally.

Pay attention to behavior, not words. Behavior has already shown there is a trust issue. You cannot trust words.

Often a confession is not what it appears to be. To determine whether the confession is a cleansing of the soul or just nastiness, decide which of the following applies to your partner:

- Your partner is a moral person who can no longer tolerate the lie and wants the relationship to end.
- Your partner is an uncaring, insensitive person.

Uncovering Deception

- Your partner and paramour have decided it's time to make a move.
- Your partner is finding it inconvenient to skulk around so s/he might as well tell.
- Your partner is actually crying out for help with issues in the relationship.
- Your partner is acting cruelly.

One through six boil down to three types of confessions. Your spouse may be confessing:

- To make the exit easier
- To repair the marriage
- To continue the lie by telling you the affair is over when it's not

You will soon find out the truth: You've taken charge by uncovering evidence and can be alert to further evidence. You need to settle down, because time and your partner's behavior will give you all the information you need.

If you determine that your partner is a cruel, uncaring person, finds it inconvenient to continue the affair in secret or plans a move out of the relationship, you may be devastated by the nastiness, but you will have clear information and should begin to plan your move.

Regardless of words your partner is not going to take you into consideration. You must take care of yourself and your family emotionally and financially. The longer you wait, worry and despair, the less control you have. Your inaction allows your partner to take control.

A confession meant to cleanse the soul, a cry for help, is obviously a different matter than a revelation meant to stun and control you. However, just because a partner confesses, all is not well. Don't roll over and play dead, agreeing everything is okay now.

If your partner has always been a trustworthy person, and you are focusing on that, **STOP IT!** Until you know exactly what you are dealing with, tread carefully. Hopefully, there will be opportunities to work through issues and make changes, but don't fall back into old behavior or blindly accept infidelity as a simple mistake. On the other hand, rushing out of the relationship is not smart. It pays to see a therapist to guide you if you plan to exit the relationship.

Section Two defines affair meanings and what you can expect if the affair was meant to repair the relationship. After the confession, the first order of business is to protect yourself legally; next, determine if the confession was meant to repair the marriage.

Saying Goodbye Isn't Simple

Life is convoluted when you devote thoughts and energy to the why, when and how of your partner's affair. You're in a war zone and don't know the enemy. Anguish and despair are palpable and overwhelming when you suspect your partner is involved in an affair. You may know you need to separate, but you simply can't seem to say goodbye. Why not? Because, at this point in time:

>Your system is in shock.
>Your ability to make an effective decision is gone.
>Your self-esteem is at zero.
>Your personal and financial security are questionable.

Loving the unfaithful person requires condemning your own behavior and making a string of excuses for the treatment you've received. You may feel your partner strayed because:

- You were emotionally unavailable.
- You didn't love enough.
- You didn't pay enough attention to your spouse.
- The other person was seductive.
- Your partner just couldn't help it.
- Your partner wanted sex and there were times you weren't available.
- You weren't attractive enough.
- You were busy with career, hobbies, sports, housework or children and should have paid more attention to your partner's needs.

Stop! Recognize that with the affair evidence you've collected your mental confusion and emotional turmoil will soon subside; you are justified in taking action.

Handling the Facts Once You Have Them

If you uncovered nothing but information that your partner is on the up-and-up and your intuition and fear have been groundless, you need help understanding yourself. Psychological issues are at work within you, distorting thoughts and feelings. Find a therapist as quickly as possible to help you unravel your confusion.

If, however, your worst fears have been confirmed, the crisis of this affair will effectively stop you in your tracks. Your normal life, ordinary thinking and planning, is gone. You no longer move from one task to another, focusing on work, errands, social events, and family responsibilities. Instead you are chained to inner-life machinations related to affair issues. In other words, your mind turns inward. Outer life focus slows.

Earlier in the book I discussed developing goals and a plan. However, the plan at this point needn't include divorce or separation. Unless your spouse has indicated s/he is out of the relationship, you have time. Do not force yourself to make the ultimate decision. Give yourself a break. You aren't settled enough, nor do you have enough facts to make a solid decision. Even if your partner has told you the relationship is over, separation and divorce take months, sometimes years; so settle in for the long haul.

Your job, while you are in crisis, is to gather information, not to determine your future. At this moment, continuously and studiously pay attention to your partner's behavior rather than words, and learn how to quiet and manage your out-of-control feelings.

CHAPTER FOUR

OVERCOMING INNER CHAOS

HOW TO HANDLE YOUR EMOTIONS

Gaining Control

In this chapter I'm going to discuss issues related to controlling yourself when you are in affair shock.

There are some things you can control and others you cannot. You can control:

- Your feelings
- Your thinking
- Your behavior

Strength lies in taking charge of your self. You cannot control your spouse or the rest of the world.

After obtaining evidence, but before confronting or taking any action, such as divorce or separation, you need clarity of thought. You may have irrefutable evidence there is an affair but, without control of your thoughts, feelings and actions, you will have difficulty proceeding. You need to bring your emotions, thought processes and behavior under control to manage yourself and your family in the best possible manner. Mental and physical damage control occurs when you are able to pull fragmenting thoughts and feelings together.

As you sort through the evidence you've obtained, you are probably dealing with an out-of-control self and a partner who consciously or unconsciously perpetuates your confusion. Concerns, fear and anger crowd out clear thinking. You experience fear of abandonment and rejection, concern for the future, anger at your partner's deliberate lies, blame, and rage at his or her good humor in the face of your trauma.

Neither the angry, bullying, emotionally volatile style nor the overly solicitous (I love you so much and will do anything for you) method brings the adulterer back. You must establish a plan and have the strength and the power to carry it out.

What does work? You develop a plan and focus on your plan without deviation.

Though Peggy was armed with concrete evidence of Rich's affair, she was emotionally stymied and fluctuated in thought, word and deed from moment to moment.

Peggy and Rich
Peggy, a 34-year-old computer programmer, walked into her first counseling session in slow motion. Words surfaced as if she were under water. Peggy watched me carefully, explaining that when Rich left she went into shock, lost massive amounts of weight, and now had night and day terrors.

After several months of Rich's disappearing act, Peggy hired a private detective. Rich would leave home for an hour "filling his gas tank;" be gone two hours running up to the drug store; or, at the end of his work day, suddenly discover he had to work late. Finally Rich moved out of the marital home, just

Overcoming Inner Chaos

to "clear his head." The truth was that Rich had another woman.

Despite the detective's information of betrayal, Peggy could not get herself under control. One day she despised Rich and planned a divorce. Just as quickly she would collapse into him with adoring love. Peggy's mind and a yo-yo were indistinguishable.

Peggy's body sagged as she talked, "I know I'm feeling and acting crazy. That scares me, but I can't help it. Rich has another woman: his secretary. But Rich continues to tell me, 'No way.' I hired a private investigator, and he's documented the other woman on video.

"Rich was furious when I told him. He stormed around the house yelling, 'You had no right. How dare you? Whose money did you use? You trumped this whole thing up.'

"I get caught up in what he's saying and turn on myself. I feel like I'm wrong. I almost feel that if I believe him, everything will be OK. His half-truths and outright lies encourage me to expect him back, though I know he's probably lying. I'm split: The believer in me wants to think everything is going to be alright, the unbeliever knows we're going down the tubes."

Managing Anger

Peggy understands Rich doesn't value honesty, yet she hesitates to call him a liar. She confuses herself with ineffective and half-hearted confrontations. She perpetuates the deception.

People who deceive others are surprised, indignant and angry when their version of the truth is confronted.

The anger is a bogus but powerful tactic used to put the recipient of the lie on the defensive. Self-righteous anger is part and parcel of the lie charade. Peggy is confused when faced with Rich's indignant anger. The power of his emotions divert the issue for Peggy from Rich's affair to managing her own out-of-control feelings.

In some ways Rich's anger soothes Peggy. If he is angry when she questions his story, maybe he is telling the truth. Of course, he's lied before, and Peggy discovered she was right. But she doesn't gain strength or confidence from that knowledge. She remains confused. "Why does he lie to me?" she asks, as though his dishonesty has something to do with her. Peggy takes Rich's lies personally: She has failed. In other words, she feels responsible for Rich's lie. Taking responsibility for another person's lies puts Peggy in a powerless position.

Blame is another tactic that diverts issue solutions. Rather than focusing on the immediate issue, determining the problem and looking for a solution, blame twists the problem into personal pokes and prods, finally disarming any solution effort. For example, Rich admonishes Peggy, "How dare you hire a detective."

When Peggy confronts Rich with detective "facts," he self-righteously attacks her: **She** did something **to him**. This suggests he is not responsible. In fact, he blames her by saying she let him down. When Peggy jumps for the bait, rather than sticking with the issue, she continues the circular, dead-ended talk. Worse, she ends up as the scapegoat. By defending herself, she implies she is to blame.

Peggy is in a bind, not only with Rich's behavior, but with powerful emotions of her own which need an outlet. What do you do with anger when you're in a no-win situation? If you express your feelings, you feel out of control because your feelings are not acknowledged. Expressing your emotions further disintegrates the situation. Yet, if you don't express yourself, you feel you will explode.

There are times when anger feels like it has a life of its own. Peggy's bottled anger leaks out despite every effort to be nice, peaceful and accepting. Her tone of voice, her body language, her lack of control, her overemotional response to a benign situation are Rich's clues that his manipulations are working.

Changing Tactics

Since Rich's words do not match his deeds, and since what he does is objectionable, there is no need to get to the ultimate truth. With a liar there is no ultimate truth. Everything slips and slides. Peggy must look to herself for solutions.

Peggy's behavior is part of the problem, but she has the power to change that behavior. If I understand I am acting in unfruitful ways, I can change. If I expect the other person to change, I'm powerless.

Peggy decided her immediate plan was to stick to her guns. She would:

- Quit asking questions (no matter how forceful the thought that she needed an answer from Rich).

- Stop calling Rich at work or at his apartment.

- Change her affect when, at 7:00 PM every night, her brooding depression began. She would take her daughters for a walk around the block, go to the store, visit a neighbor, see a friend or exercise.

Checking Credibility

When you are confused by your own thoughts and feelings, it is appropriate to proceed with caution and in a way that promises to resolve the ambivalence you feel about your situation. Begin by looking at your interactions and determine if your style of acting-in with a liar or reacting with anger has destroyed your own credibility.

Destroying Credibility: You destroy your credibility by acting over and over in opposition to your verbalizations. Examples could include saying: "I won't stand for this," and then you do stand for it; or "I don't believe anything you say," then acting as if you believe by taking lies seriously. Probing and asking questions of a known liar make you foolish and sets the stage for more lies.

Reestablishing Credibility: Create consistency between your behavior in speech, in emotions and in attitude. Your credibility begins with trusting yourself and planning your behavior. While you're deciding what you want for your relationship and for your future, set limits for yourself and establish your credibility. This gives you strength and power. You are powerless when you keep asking questions, when you say one thing but do another, when you make exceptions and allow impulses to overwhelm you. Set limits for yourself in areas you can control. Start small, then move on to more determinative behavior. Some examples of setting various limits might include:

Small limit: Time is concrete, if you say dinner is at 6:00 PM, and your partner agrees, you proceed with dinner at 6:00 PM, whether or not your partner is there.

Medium limit: Discussing issues only if time, length and subject of talk have been agreed upon.

Large limit : If you decide to divorce, it cannot be mere talk or threat. You must take action. You must establish *yourself.*

Gaining Control of Your Emotions: What to Expect and How to React

The trauma of an affair shocks and damages mind and body, just as a serious auto accident would. The mental and emotional trauma affects physical functioning. You lose weight and can't sleep; your stomach is in knots; your intestines malfunction; your heart flutters; your breathing is shallow; your immunity to illness declines.

These physical symptoms will right themselves once your thoughts are in order. You can help yourself adapt to affair-shock by understanding and expecting the tremendous devastation an affair takes on body, mind and emotions.

When you know what to expect, you can take charge of your feelings. Expect yourself to go through three emotional phases:

1. Fugue
2. Ambivalence
3. Mourning/Acceptance

Fugue

The first phase, Fugue, brings mind-stopping, staggering, incredible fear; anxiety and raging jealousy. Your mind and nerves are on fire. You feel abandoned and wonder why, when and how this happened to you. You wonder, "What did I do? What should I have done?" You are either withdrawn and mute, or you can't shut up.

Fugue is the first phase of affair-trauma. Mind and emotions are out of control. Your feelings fluctuate wildly; chaos reigns in your mind, heart, soul and spirit.

SYMPTOMS OF FUGUE INCLUDE:

- Despair, disbelief and denial—You grapple with broken trust, your mind can't seem to grasp reality.

- Depression and confusion--You feel staggering fear moving in and out of your consciousness.

- Anxiety and raging jealousy--You think your mind and nerves are on fire.

- Abandonment--You feel deserted, constantly wondering Who, Why, When, How?

- Responsibility--You question what you have done or should have done.

- Withdrawal--You cannot sleep. You are either mute, or you can't shut up.

You don't feel free to express any of these feelings or experiences to your partner, yet they leak out. You may be sickeningly sweet--loving totally and completely. Or, you may rage--demanding answers, shouting and wailing your devastation and humiliation. Your partner may concur s/he's been a louse. S/he's sorry she hurt you, she didn't mean it. "It just happened," she says.

Now your spouse has absolved himself by being sorry and empathic, but the problem has not gone away.

Instead your out-of-control behavior turns **you** into the problem, the person to be handled and managed.

Raging and wailing solve nothing. You may feel temporary relief which turns sour in a moment. You wonder, "Why did I do that? I've turned negative thoughts about me into reality." With that you sink back into abysmal dejection.

Your behavior gives her or him a reprieve. Like a child who has been spanked, either your partner has evened the score for the affair, or feels justified saying, "See, this person is so difficult to live with, no wonder I'm having an affair!"

Out-of-control emotions, angry recriminations and blame are predictable, natural responses to an affair. But they are seldom helpful, and they do not alleviate the problem.

When you know what you are up against, what is natural, you will move on more quickly to healing. Just as your body needs time to recover from injury, your emotions also need time to heal the affair trauma.

Fugue will end, and you will be in stage two: Ambivalence.

Ambivalence

While in phase I, Fugue, thoughts about the affair and the other woman or man throw you into a dimension of intense emotions which either squeeze and compress you so tightly you can't breath, or make you feel you're loose, falling apart and fragmented. Feelings run amok.

In the second phase, Ambivalence, you begin to accept reality. An affair is in process. Your thoughts, feelings and actions flounder--flopping from one mind set to another.

SYMPTOMS OF AMBIVALENCE:

- Anguish versus anger--One minute you are crying and sobbing; the next, you're ready to kill.

- Frustration versus fear paralysis—You continuously stir the pot with nasty words and sarcasm or find yourself afraid to say or do anything.

- Humiliation versus pride--You vacillate between being ashamed and guilty, and feeling blameless and innocent.

- Obsessive thoughts versus blanking out--You swing between desperately needing details and refusing to think about the affair.

- Hope versus throwing in the towel--One moment you think s/he really loves you; the next the relationship's over.

- Intolerance versus accepting affair behavior--Your moods swing from saccharine sweet, loving and sexual to disgust, repulsion, and a desire to eliminate this person from your life.

Mourning and acceptance

You gradually move to the next stage; Mourning and Acceptance. This stage involves both grief and action. The historical relationship is gone--with sadness and your blessing. You are a survivor; wiser, growing and developing as you let go of the past.
During this stage you will cycle through the following feelings.

SYMPTOMS OF MOURNING AND ACCEPTANCE

Mourning--The relationship is gone; interest in life is gone.

- Feeling sadness or loss--You are grieving or emotionless.

- Taking action--You decide to let go, either forgive or divorce.

- Achieving peace--You own yourself.

Each phase feels as if it is forever. It isn't. You will change. You will grow. In the meantime, don't brutalize yourself. Remember, these are normal stages through affair trauma. That means you have the right and power to let go and change or to continue to be tormented.

Controlling Your Thoughts

To get through the trauma of each affair phase requires concentration and fortitude. You have been blind-sided by infidelity. You have every reason to be overwhelmed by depression, anxiety and fear. You have a right to take to your bed for six months. But, what you need to do is **PULL YOURSELF TOGETHER. IMMEDIATELY.**
Concentrate on freeing your mind from affair details and questions moment by moment, (not for all time, not for an hour, only for this moment), moving the thoughts of the betrayer out. Establish a method to control what goes on and stick to it. You can't change your partner or the situation. Time will change your feelings but, in the meantime, you have to take charge of yourself.
Desire for change that has to do with your spouse's change is self-defeating. H/she is separate. H/she is unavailable. At this moment can you change this person?

No. Can you change yourself? Yes. You start by controlling your mind one moment at a time. Live in this moment. Take charge of this moment.

The most important person to think about and take care of is you. It is imperative you settle down and think clearly. Only through clear thinking can you protect both short and long term interests.

Right this moment change your thoughts. Thoughts change emotions. Your emotional state includes any or all of the feelings listed above. When you begin falling into mental and emotional chaos, change your state by taking charge of yourself. **Stop your thought and change it,** tell yourself:

1. Feelings are not facts.

2. I can only change myself.

3. Nasty, mean thoughts need not be spoken.

4. I am powerful, not powerless.

5. I will control the actions which lead to my emotional turmoil; I am accountable for my actions just as my partner is.

6. Life is not fair.

Change takes practice. The more you manage your thoughts and emotions, the more control you will have. You are honing mental skills just as an athlete hones physical skills.

Just because a thought comes to mind or an emotion sweeps over you does not mean you must take the emotional hit, zero in and ruminate on the thought.

Your job is to save yourself and turn a devastating situation into a growth experience. The situation you're in makes you feel powerless. On the contrary, you are powerful, and the more you exercise your mind and manage emotions the more powerful you become.

Taking Action Physically and Mentally

An excellent way to change is by turning thoughts into action. If you are free to do so, run in place, do jumping jacks, run around the block, jump rope, get in the shower and scream, walk two miles, write in your journal, make a list about controlling behavior.

I know you don't feel like it; you barely have motivation to drag yourself out of bed. Just as you brush your teeth or take a shower whether you like it or not, you must take action to take control.

Any desire that has to do with your partner taking action is self defeating. Your partner is separate and unavailable. At this exact moment in time can you change him? No. Can you change yourself? Yes.

Work on changing your thoughts. Work on changing your feelings. Your perception determines behavior and feelings. Acknowledge those feelings and thoughts, then let go and empty your mind of depressing negative ideas. Start with control one moment at a time. Live in that moment, take charge of that moment. Follow these steps:

1. Develop confidence. The moment you realize you are anxious and depressed: Stop! You've been telling yourself you can't bear the situation. **YOU CAN.**

2. Focus on this moment. Is there anything you can do about your partner or the situation this moment? No. *Stop focusing on painful thoughts.*

3. Change your physical state. If you cry in bed, get up. **GO OUTSIDE**. Write a letter, write about your feelings, the situation and, most importantly, what you want for yourself.

4. Wallow in your feelings for one minute. Time yourself. Then take action. Exercise. Walk. Run. Do aerobics, floor exercises, jump rope.

5. Structure your day hour by hour. If necessary, structure it 15 minutes at a time. Keep your plan in front of you, constantly refer to it and stick to the plan.

6. Keep track of how often you think of your mate and the affair. Map it out as if you are setting up a study. Facts bring thought patterns into consciousness and allow you to alter or eliminate problem thinking.

Changing your state may be more difficult at work: Self-consciousness may be a problem. "What will coworkers think?" Guessing others' thoughts is magical thinking. You are in crisis and you need to change your thoughts and feelings. Jump up from your desk, suck in your stomach, walk to the bathroom, drink cold water, stroll down the hall, around the plant or around your desk. Imagine yourself wrapped in an invisible opaque balloon, no one can see you. Don't let self-consciousness stop your progress.

No one knows what's going on in your mind. Other people's thoughts are just that--other people's thoughts. If your behavior disturbs them, it's their problem.

Emotional and mental self-control is critical to a successful outcome

You are in crisis. Crisis is the beginning of greater understanding of yourself and your interpersonal relationships. You will gradually gain control of emotions, thoughts and actions.

Managing emotions and thoughts puts you in a calm position to determine actions which are in your best interest. Recognizing what type of affair your partner is having also guides your eventual decision to be in or out of the relationship.

SECTION TWO

AFFAIRS FALL INTO THREE CATEGORIES

CHAPTER FIVE

The Bridge Affair

**Determining the Affair Type:
Self-serving, Repair or Bridge**

The betrayer often says when discovered, "It didn't mean a thing." Wrong! An affair results in profound and long-lasting consequences to a relationship whether the affair is a one-night stand or a year long romance.

Although no two affairs are exactly alike, they all share similar characteristics. Once you understand what your partner's affair means, you will be in a better position to take charge of yourself and the situation, and to plan ahead.

Emotional investment in an affair differs from the casual sexual fling to the long-term, romantic love affair. Affair meanings go from "Help, this marriage is in serious trouble," to "So long, this marriage is over."

Understanding the purpose of your partner's affair is part of the solution. Your partner may not value monogamy (or may not have values) and flits from one sexual conquest to another. Or the affair may be an unconscious process to solve marital problems. It may also be an easy on your spouse way out of the marriage.

In this chapter I start with a broad explanation of three affair categories, then discuss the bridge affair at length (Chapter 5 and Chapter 6 discuss self-serving and repair affairs).

There are three affair categories:

- The self-serving affair
- The repair affair
- The bridge affair

The Self-serving Affair

In the self-serving affair the straying partner seeks to elevate self-esteem and to find sexual satisfaction or enhancement.

People who initiate self-serving affairs are narcissists. They move in a world of mirrors, empathic only to themselves. They focus their attention only on those people who will glorify and amplify the narcissist's own image. These people are busy proving to themselves and others they are desired sexually.

The havoc their **philandering** creates doesn't affect them. They not only deny their behavior is a problem, they view sexual liaisons as nothing more than distractions.

The Repair Affair and the Bridge Affair

A **repair affair** is designed to create a crisis which gets the full attention of a spouse. It says something is dramatically wrong with the marriage and provides an opportunity to repair the bond.

The bridge affair acts as a bridge out of the marriage. Individuals initiating bridge affairs want to leave their marriages but need lovers to help "hand-hold" them out, guaranteeing departure from the marital relationship.

Repair affairs and bridge affairs are meant to solve relationship problems; the first by restoring or re-forming the relationship, the second by ending the relationship.

The Bridge Out

You realize your partner is emotionally gone. You know what should be done but feel immobilized. Chuck, in the case study below, is an excellent example. Although Karrie's affair was quickly terminated, she never returned emotionally and intimately to their marriage. Her affair was a bridge affair--a bridge out of the relationship

Chuck, a gas station operator, married Karrie when he was 24. Because of his age and lack of experience, he had trouble understanding relationships and personalities.

Chuck and Karrie
Both Karrie and Chuck wanted marriage counseling to determine whether their marriage could be saved. Each indicated that marriage and family were their top priorities.

In the first session 31-year-old Karrie, a nurse, spoke as though Chuck wasn't in the room, "I just fell into the affair. Steve wanted me. I don't know why. He's so handsome, so sexy, so personable and nice. All my friends love him and talk about how sexy he is. I'm just...you see...nothing to look at, no shape, no nothing! Now I realize that to Steve, our affair was all about sex.

When asked how he felt about what his wife said, Chuck's response to Karrie's lack of empathy was, "I'm glad she's honest." He seemed proud that he could listen without flinching.

Karrie continued, "I was right to tell him it's over, wasn't I? I saw him yesterday, and when he didn't look at me I felt sick. I wanted to rush over and take all my words back. I really don't want to do the right thing. It doesn't feel right to me."

Karrie's affair began when Steve pursued her. Steve was the soccer coach for the team on which Karrie and Chuck's daughter played. He paid inordinate amounts of attention to Karrie when the other kids and parents were around, and he called her at home, "just to chat." Karrie was flattered and surprised.

She didn't mention the calls to Chuck, but when he saw a tube of lubricant protruding from Karrie's purse, he stared unbelieving. He had never known Karrie to be interested in sex. Though Chuck was scared and suspicious, he decided not to ask about what he saw.

In therapy both Karrie and Chuck agreed that open communication was not one of their strengths. Chuck said he "knew enough" not to bother asking if there was another person.

Instead, Chuck began recording his wife's phone conversations and soon had confirmation of his suspicions.

When Chuck confronted Karrie with proof, she confessed and informed her lover that Chuck knew about their affair. Karrie felt forced to end the affair but said, "It broke my heart."

Instead of feeling sorrow for Chuck's pain or using the affair to focus on and strengthen their marriage, Karrie turned her affair into punishment for Chuck through distancing, anger, disgust and loss of respect for him.

Karrie's behavior was a clear statement that she no longer valued the marriage. However, she talked out of both sides of her mouth. One day she'd tell Chuck she wanted him and the family; the next she was no longer interested.

Chuck stayed confused, loving Karrie one moment and hating her the next, regularly berating himself and taking responsibility for her behavior, "If I'd been a better husband she wouldn't have done it."

Karrie showed him she was not trustworthy and then treated him with disdain. Although Karrie wasn't nasty every moment, her behavior was unacceptable often enough to be viewed as fact. Yet, Chuck was not able to take Karrie's behavior seriously and let go.

Karrie's affair was a bridge out of the relationship. Her behavior following the affair indicated she was not working on the marriage nor was she empathic with Chuck's pain.

Two years after Chuck discovered the affair, Karrie divorced him. It took over a year in therapy for Chuck to grasp the fact that his wife was as she appeared, not as he imagined her.

Death of the Marital Relationship

The bridge affair is a bridge out of the marriage--the death of the marital relationship. The purpose of a bridge affair is to escape the marriage by finding a new partner and avoiding the confrontation of marital problems.

Individuals involved in bridge affairs have abandoned commitment to their marriages. They may have lost touch and cannot communicate with their partners, or they may be constantly arguing and fighting.

Unable to be honest or take responsibility for the desire to leave the marriage, these individuals begin an underground offensive. They unconsciously, sometimes consciously, use an extramarital affair to force the issue. Their aim is to force their spouse into either leaving or insisting they leave.

This behavior allows individuals initiating bridge affairs to hold their partners, or the individuals with whom they are involved, responsible, as the cause of relationship deterioration. Such a strategy does not always work, since some partners will not end the marriage. In that case the individual having the affair decides to leave to relieve the tension, have time to think, or separate and work on the marriage. Although bogus, these excuses are grasped eagerly by the abandoned partner.

There are also those people whose lives are incomplete without mates, to whom being alone is unbearable. They cannot tolerate being alone even for brief spans of time. They must be attached before they can detach, regardless of the misery they cause.

The bridge-out-of-the-marriage affair is an escape route which does not solve marital problems nor does it confront the spouse.

Determining if the Affair Signals Marital Departure

The bridge affair is painful from start to finish, since the end result is separation and divorce. Both you and your partner deny the serious consequences of the affair. Denial is the cornerstone experience when dealing with a bridge affair.

Denial protects your partner from your wrath. It also buys time for the partner to determine a plan and establish a rhythm while crossing the bridge. For a time

The Bridge Affair

denial keeps the pain of rejection and abandonment at bay for you, but it actually prolongs processing reality.

You may pick up on a secret bridge affair subliminally. Your sensory perception antennae quiver as you sense the affair and understand what is happening without conscious confirmation. Such sensing is like an animal sniffing the air, ears at attention, hairs standing on end, waiting, uneasy. You know something's different, something's wrong. You ask your spouse, "How are you feeling, is everything all right?" Since the response is that all is well, you are temporarily relieved; the threat diminishes; the fear subsides.

Still, your mind scurries around looking for answers but keeps running into a dead end. You are mind-isolated because you're not a mind reader, and your partner verbally reveals nothing.

At this point, follow your intuition. If a month or two passes and you still feel "something" is amiss, take it seriously. Your desire to avoid investigating, to deny the issue won't resolve the problem. *You need to take charge in any way you possibly can*.

If an affair isn't the problem, excellent, no harm done. If your spouse confronts you, accusing you of being suspicious, graciously acknowledge it and present the evidence--your intuition. Your partner may take umbrage or feel distressed about your investigation. However, it serves notice. It lets your partner know your relationship means too much to you to stand by and do nothing.

In the following bridge affair, Charles first denied there was a problem, then blamed Megan for their problems. At the same time he suggested he had never been happy with her. Finally, he confessed. He was having an affair. Megan was incredulous and in shock. It took her months, actually a year-and-a-half, to feel secure and confident in her decision that ending the marriage was the correct thing to do.

There are a few exceptions, but the majority of women long for relationships. Many women dream about the perfect man who will love and care for them, be a companion and provide security. For this woman, having her own man is a powerful necessity, like water. She has to be in love with her own man. It begins in adolescence. The need courses through her veins, pounds through her heart and soul. Having her personal man is as much a need as breathing. She searches, looking for him. She feels unfulfilled, is often miserable until she finds him.

This woman's happiness and satisfaction is dependent upon intimate connection with her man. She is totally absorbed in him; the world revolves around him. This is her relationship dream state.

Megan was one of those women: For her, her husband's affair meant not only displacement but disappearance of the self.

Megan and Charles

Megan's light brown hair, flecked with gray, capped her face with a buoyant, springy alive-look in contrast to her depressed face and sagging body. Stressed by life and her first therapy session, Megan appeared looking anxious and exhausted.

Megan, a 47-year-old housewife, lived vicariously through her husband, Charles, the 48-year-old president of a computer supply company. She hosted business parties and dinners, accompanied her husband to out of town sales meetings, and took an active role in their country club, which was paid for by the company and considered a business perk. Her life centered around Charles' interests and business.

The Bridge Affair

In therapy Megan said, "I've lost 35 pounds recently so these," she pulled at her slacks, "don't fit.

"I've also been sick with a number of viruses. I'm dehydrated that's why I have this Evian bottle with me and have no appetite. My doctor wants to put me in the hospital, but I won't let him," she looked straight at me, "At least I'm able to make one decision.

"My problem is my husband, Charles. He's confessed he had an affair," Megan put her head down during a long pause and said quietly, "and I'm not sure it's over." She looked up and asked, "Is there a way to tell? I thought you might be able to tell me how to ask him the right questions or figure out by what he's said, just what's going on with him. If I knew for sure, I'd feel better. I asked him about marriage counseling. He said we can resolve our own problems.

"All this trouble started in November when his company had their annual holiday dinner dance. We had no sooner walked in, deposited our coats and chatted with a few of Charles' co-workers when Loretta, one of his assistants, slithered up to us--you can tell I despise her--and the two of them disappeared for 30 minutes.

"I was embarrassed to be left alone, but I was also furious, I kept thinking: What a jerk! What does he imagine other people are thinking? At the time I didn't view it as serious, in terms of an affair, that is.

"Later Charles explained to me that Loretta had something important to discuss regarding one of their clients. And I bought it. I felt uneasy, but Charles and I have always been tight. I mean anyone we know would tell you that we have always had one of the most solid marriages around."

Megan sat on the edge of the couch. As she talked, she nervously pushed at her cuticles. "I guess the point I'm trying to make is that I now know Charles has been sexually involved with Loretta. I'm upset all the time. I'm mad. I'm sad. I wake up off and on all night and my immediate thought is about his affair. I can't believe it."

Every man involved with another woman says, "I'm just not happy," or, "I'm not sure I love you any more," and totally denies having an affair.

Charles used another old standby when Megan asked what was wrong. He said, "I don't know, must be mid-life crisis."

Charles exited the marital relationship and is emotionally attached to the other woman. However, he was afraid to tell Megan the truth. "The Lie" has become his life. His mind is focused on the other woman and his life with Megan is peripheral.

Megan feels the lie, knows it, but wants to believe the deception. She wants to maintain status quo. She denies what she knows and makes excuses for Charles: His job is stressful, he's worried about money, parents, children. She's intent on dredging up anything as a possible explanation that the affair is temporary, an aberration for Charles.

Charles' affair has catapulted Megan into another dimension. The integrity of her life is fragmented. Megan can no longer feel safe or secure. She is no longer under the umbrella of Charles' power.

Recognizing Critical Bridge Words

When a bridge affair is exposed and the marriage is over, your partner will do just as Charles did.

This information is critical. A bridge affair is in process when your partner:

1. Does not say, "I'm sorry. I was stupid."

2. Does not say, "S/he's gone. I won't see him or her or talk to that person again." (Time will tell you if this statement is fact.)

3. Does not say, "I love you. I want the marriage."

4. Does not put extraordinary time into listening to you, reassuring you s/he is there for you.

5. Confesses sexual involvement without heartfelt shame or sorrow.

6. Says, "I'm not sure I ever loved you."

7. Implies you have not grown and developed, you are stunted, the affair is your fault.

At the same time your partner is considering leaving, you may hear, "I'll always love you. I'll always take care of you." In these cases, I recommend worry.

Your partner may also talk about the future, subtly encouraging you to think you have one together. Beware. Such statements may be solely intended to buy time and cool you out.

Bridge Affair Lies

Charles escaped marital confrontation and problems as he moved into another life by lying. He didn't say, "I'm sorry, our marriage is over." Instead, he continued his life of deception by denying anything serious was happening.

When confronted with evidence Charles continued to lie. Up against the wall of detection, he switched to justifying his infidelity by saying, "It just happened." In effect, he portrayed himself as an innocent bystander swept away by circumstances beyond his control.

Instead of being honest he began an underground offensive. He presented himself as puzzled, questioning the marital relationship and his commitment. He called his actions a mid-life crisis to avoid addressing the real issues and underlying problems in the marriage. In truth, Charles depended on Megan's intolerance of his behavior to propel him out of the marriage.

The person involved in an affair almost always denies that it has been sexual even when they admit they've been seeing another person. They try to evade the consequences of their betrayal to the bitter end. "Never, ever, admit it, even if there are pictures!" Once a clandestine sexual relationship exists the marital contract/commitment is broken.

Processing the Meaning of a Bridge Affair

Megan wants to know, "What does Charles' affair mean?" As his partner, but without access to his mind, she scrambles to grasp the depth of the problem. At the same time, Charles is irritable and tense. He insists Megan is making too much of the affair. He participates in family life, takes care of Megan, the children and the house in a perfunctory manner. His "self" is not available, he is no longer fully present. As Megan senses Charles' withdrawal, he denies her questions which he interprets as accusations.

Megan, meanwhile, in emotional shock and denial, is unable to integrate reality. She describes herself as "vibrating" with anxiety and feeling disorientated. Time has slowed down. What once took five minutes now takes two hours. Her concentration is gone. She can't think clearly and continually questions why Charles did or said what he did.

She wishes she had loved more, spoken the right words or acted differently. Megan describes herself: "I've gone from whistling and singing my way through life into a sinkhole so black I'm lost. Nothing makes sense. This sounds crazy but I don't feel like I'm alive."

Until Megan moves into a more stable mind set, the meaning of her husband's affair is too threatening. She has to take the time to process and digest the magnitude of change it brings into her life. Emotionally, Charles is light-years ahead of her; Megan has to catch up.

The transition from devoted family person to involvement with another is slow and subtle. The person having an affair moves slowly into an affair membrane, shrugging off questions or suggestions that something's wrong, is deliberately discreet about mental and physical activities.

Grasping Reality and Changing

Megan slowly acknowledged reality and as she did, was able to think about her future and what she needed. There were still times when she fell back, pulling at Charles to resume their life together. A roller-coaster period of depression and anger overwhelmed her as she recognized her situation: forty-nine-years old with no work skills or experience.

Finally, Megan was done with Charles, in fact, happy he was gone. At the same time she decided to go to college or enter a training program both to stimulate herself and prepare for the future. Intellectually she had accepted his departure for months, but emotionally she hadn't let go.

Today she feels good. She has surrounded herself with interesting women and an occasional non-serious man. Her life is totally different.

If a marriage is terminated precipitously, either longing for the partner or bitterness may continue for months, sometimes years. Charles' difficulty taking action actually helped Megan. It gave her time to let go.

Rationale for the Bridge Affair

Bridge affairs occur for a variety of reasons. The connection between partners emotionally, intellectually and physically, may be dying or may have been dead for months, even years. Long-term frustration or momentary needs often begin bridge affairs as a means to fulfill sexual desires, express anger or punish the spouse. However, an affair begun in such a fashion can turn into a bridge out of the marriage.

Sometimes a bridge affair is begun when a partner seeks sexual fulfillment. The need for sexual fulfillment occurs when sex is missing in the marriage in the quality and quantity required. Tension and pressure are caused by too few sexual encounters and/or there is lack of desire due to tension and pressure. Sexual life with the "affairee" may develop into true intimacy and love.

Other bridge affairs begin as a result of anger or frustration; an attempt to balance power that has shifted

The Bridge Affair

or as a tactic to boost self-esteem that has been beaten down. Choosing another person is seldom consciously based on, "I'll show her." Rather, it most often is a means to soothe the self.

A third type of affair can begin when a partner seeks to punish a spouse. In such affairs, the partner believes s/he is right, the spouse is wrong, any misdeed is intolerable. Punishment, meted out for a perceived lack of caring or incompetence, involves emotional abuse, criticism or the silent treatment. The ultimate punishment is choosing another person, covertly threatening, and finally overtly threatening and carrying out divorce.

Regardless of bridge affair rationale, the emotional connection with the spouse has dissipated or disappeared and the adulterer, rather than face issues and problems, has chosen the easy way out.

Determining What To Do When Your Partner Is Bridging Out

Picture your partner walking over a bridge, the bridge disappearing behind her/him and your partner is gone.

Yes, it is painful. As quickly as possible, you need intellectually to grasp the futility of your connection. It's important to bring your intellect up to speed. Expect your emotions will drag behind your intellect and catch up later.

There is no chance for a relationship to survive when you are with a person who can't commit love and the future to you. Your spouse's dance around a firm and steadfast commitment is concrete information that your partner is with you in body only and even that body is part-time.

A bridge affair equals separation: You are on one side; your spouse on the other.

CHAPTER SIX

RECOGNIZING THE SELF-SERVING AFFAIR

PHILANDERING: A MARITAL ADJUNCT

To philander is "to love insincerely" according to *Webster's Dictionary of the American Language.* Philanderers seek excitement and avoid commitment by moving from one partner to another. They achieve temporary fulfillment through variety or conquest. They require a steady stream of new partners, each viewed as a prize, a thing, property.

Although legally married, philanderers act and feel unattached and uncommitted. They move from woman to woman or man to man without guilt or empathy for their spouse.

When an affair is discovered, the philanderer verbalizes guilt and sorrow--primarily to get through the crisis of discovery, meanwhile leaving a path of broken hearts and chaos.

Discovering the Affair

When the affair is revealed, philanderers typically want to maintain marriages while they continue to add spice to their lives with a variety of partners.

The Self Serving Affair

In other cases the marriage may continue because the philanderer's partner chooses to adapt for reasons of family, dependency or masochistic necessity. Nevertheless, the fragile connection, if there was one, is broken.

People who light-heartedly dally in affairs do not seek deep, close, intimate relationships with anyone; not spouse, children, lovers, or co-workers. Relationships are superficial. Since the philanderer's commitment is shallow, you might feel you should be able to shrug off knowledge of the affair quickly. Not so. An affair goes to the core of your being.

This brings us to attachment theory which describes men and women who philander as people who cannot attach. They fear closeness, are self-contained and alienated emotionally from others as well as from themselves. Because they are marriage adjuncts, self-serving or dalliance affairs are not meant to disrupt the marital status quo.

Core elements of attachment and love--the feeling that somebody is emotionally there for you, someone you can connect with, another person who will respond to you, particularly if you are in need--are the same for children and adults. A good, intimate adult relationship requires two people who can experience feelings of vulnerability, being scared, feel overwhelmed by life, at times be unsure of who they are. It is a safe place where a partner responds to these needs, allows you to sense the world as home rather than as a dangerous place.

We all need other people to help us process our emotions and deal with the slings and arrows of being alive. To be decimated by the arrow of your partner's affair reverberates to the core of your being and you cannot be comforted.

A light-hearted affair is demeaning and diminishing. It is intolerable when repeated. It robs a person of security and comfort. When you discover or even suspect an affair-

-whether it is the first or third, the effect is profound. You can't sleep or eat. You feel emotionally crippled, questioning the meaning of the affair and the depth of involvement. Attachment is gone, your love bond broken, and security disappears.

Recognizing Self-serving Affairs as Marriage Adjuncts

The self-serving affair is a marriage adjunct or supplement, a filler for what is viewed as unavailable at home, or for a perceived lack in your partner. The deficit, however, is not with you; it is within the person having the affair. Such people are without insight. They are not able to blame themselves or even look inside. Any difficulties life presents come from outside themselves.

For philanderers, infidelity is viewed as part of life, a search for fun and games. Their creed is "One woman or man is not enough or good enough for me."

Since philanderers view infidelity as a part of life, these individuals feel little guilt and blame. They may verbalize guilt or report feeling sorry when confronted or caught, but their words are meaningless. They are back at the dalliance game as soon as the coast is clear.

Searching for Variety, Excitement and Conquest

A male philanderer may be a "macho" man who values men's power and men's pursuits, making any attachment shallow and time-limited. These men stay with women who take care of them but continue tandem involvements throughout their lives. (Yes, there are women who understand their husbands have wandering eyes but accept the behavior since these men always come home to them.)

The female philanderer who involves herself in light-hearted affairs cannot attach. She views people as objects, like a chair. Eventually she finds the chair uninteresting, boring. She becomes tired of the color or the fabric and decides, "I need a replacement."

For self servers, the intimate emotional loop binding partners together is missing. Instead the loop is a fragile string which can be snapped in two for any reason at any time.

When a philanderer loses interest in his or her spouse, the dullness of the relationship is within the individual. It has nothing to do with pain in the relationship or with excuses such as, "I was never happy" or "I'm not sure I ever loved you." Nor can the individual zero in on a particular point in time in the relationship which marks a crucial turning point in feelings for the spouse.

The philanderer says to the therapist, "I felt restless," and to the spouse, "The affair means nothing, it just happened. I love you. Something is wrong with me." In one aspect, the philanderer is right. Although meant as an excuse, the explanation means nothing. It's simply a maneuver to maintain the marital relationship and promote the idea of impersonal action.

Sandy's need to roam was never-ending, in spite of her marital state. Sandy called her infidelity a "personality quirk which hurt no one." In fact, she smiled and laughed at her cleverness. Sandy had fun, particularly when a relationship began, but the laughs and giggles were short-lived for her partner.

Sandy

When Sandy was a little girl she dreamed of finding Prince Charming, a handsome man, socially adept, able to make money; a man who

would adore and care for her. She fell in love with fantasy, her own dream representation. Once Sandy's fantasy of marriage became reality, Sandy discovered her dream husband and real husband didn't match.

She intended, she said, to be faithful forever. However, intention is not the same as loyalty, integrity and commitment. And Sandy could not be faithful, remain committed and attached. Thus, her fragile commitment to her husband was abandoned when she felt a powerful attraction to the coach.

Delicate looking, with black marble eyes, the 33-year-old librarian revealed in her first therapy session that she had just terminated a year long affair with the coach. She had not spoken to him nor seen him for two months but needed the therapist's help to maintain her resolve.

After six sessions I went on vacation. In the first post-vacation session Sandy confessed, "I was obsessed. I've never felt that way before, and I hope it never happens again.

"I was shaking and couldn't stop thinking about the situation. I called his wife.

"Although they had an unlisted number, I searched and prodded until I found it. I identified myself and said I wanted to talk about the coach. The coach's wife said she didn't know me and was not interested in discussing her husband. She hung up. I called back twice. Both times his wife hung up.

"Later I called to talk to the coach. He hung up three times and the next day changed his phone number."

A month later, laughing, Sandy said, "You know I definitely planned to put the brakes on, never put myself in this position of having an affair again, but oh, well, here I go. I didn't mention that I met Dave a month ago. He makes me feel alive.

"I could care less how my husband acts. He ignores me and I don't care. Without a "friend," I'd be upset and confronting him, getting into it with him. So, this is better. I have something to think about. I feel good, even though I know it's an immature high."

Therapy was Sandy's cover. She realized in therapy that she chose not to change and treatment ended.

Sandy is a shallow person unable to attach. She ignored her husband and proceeded through a number of affairs. Her husband eventually divorced her.

Who is Seducing Whom?

While Sandy was blatant and sought out male companionship, Jona viewed herself as the victim.

Jona
Tall and slim, 31-year-old Jona had the confident, long-legged stride of a tomboy. Once inside the therapy office, however, Jona broke down and sobbed, "I knew he was married and had other female friends but I didn't think it would happen to me. Now he's talking to another woman.

"He's my boss. He's married. I'm married. He's way too old for me, for heaven's sake. I don't know what's wrong with me.

"I guess my love began innocently because he was understanding. He listened to me."

Can a married woman have an "innocent" affair with a married man?

No.

Facts and track record mean nothing as the dance of seduction begins. After intimacy is established a woman says, "I knew he ran around." Yet, she is shocked when it is clear her lover is off again with another woman. Seduction experts know how to generate excitement by focusing on and acting interested in their prey. They are interested, mainly challenged, by the chance to prove once again their irresistible lure.

Why does Jona or any woman choose a philanderer? If she wins him over and he loves her, she's won. Or she may need a shallow, distant man who makes few demands and with whom she has a parallel relationship. (A parallel relationship holds little intimacy; togetherness evolves out of necessity—sex, for example.) Jona isn't an innocent bystander, although it comforts her to view herself as the victim.

Jona may be masochistic; she may unconsciously want to be emotionally beaten, humiliated and embarrassed. The other side of the coin is she may need to beat, humiliate and embarrass. The relationship is an exciting game of one-up-woman-ship.

Her relationship with her boss felt like love to Jona. John comforted her when her mother and father died in an auto accident. He was understanding, a strong shoulder to cry on in times of need. Her husband, on the other hand, told her not to cry--even at her parents' funeral. John became Jona's loving parent.

John, who was 50, understood Jona's vulnerability and emotional availability. John needed conquests and stimulation to sustain his identity as a man. Jona was vulnerable and John stepped in.

Ten months later, Jona changed. She felt ambivalent about the relationship. Still, she was not ready to let go. She and John fought when he got flowers from an "old friend." "She means nothing. Nothing's going on," John told Jona. "You're jealous and angry about nothing." To Jona it meant something, something big.

Jona wanted to believe John and did--at times. When one red rose and a card were left on his car, she told John, "That's too bold." John made excuses. In therapy Jona declared, "I believe him." Yet, in the same breath, she wondered if John took the other woman to their secret apartment.

Constantly torn, but unable to make a decision to accept John's behavior or get out of the relationship, Jona vacillated. When Jona felt strong and independent, John moved to see her more often. When Jona softened and collapsed into John, he became distant.

Therapy changed Jona, helped firm her up, strengthen her ego, and clarify her behavior and John's. Finally she accepted the fact that John received calls, cards and letters from other women. Also, she took responsibility for the fact that she had chosen John, neglected her husband and ignored her values and marriage vows.

Jona took a serious look at herself, at her values and at what she wanted from a relationship. She decided to re-examine her marital relationship with her husband and he agreed to participate. They are in process of growth and development, their marital future unknown.

We can assume John is proceeding on his path of seduction.

Personality Tendencies at the Root of Self-serving Affairs

Certain personality styles lend themselves to acting out through affairs.

The Perfectionistic Style

These are personalities who either distrust or need perfection and, therefore, find it difficult to live in a real but imperfect world with real but imperfect partners.

Perfectionists have no tolerance for other ideas, thoughts or behavior. Their theme is, "I am right. You are wrong." As punishment they use emotional abuse based on any thought that comes to mind. They belittle, criticize or put down the marital partner. They mete out punishment for being pregnant, having a baby or working ten minutes longer than usual. These individuals turn any situation in life into an example of incompetency or lack of caring.

The perfectionist chooses another person who is perfect. That person is perfect because normal idiosyncrasies or other personality difficulties have not surfaced yet.

Alienated and Dissatisfied

Alienated individuals are primitive, undeveloped people who cannot be satisfied with their partners. They are flat emotionally and self absorbed. Their job in life is caring for themselves. Paradoxically, because they lack empathy and cannot connect with others, they are doomed to dissatisfaction and engage in a series of short, transient affairs.

Adventure-seeking

Adventure is the name of the game in every arena, including sex. This individual never worries about or regrets his behavior. The adventure seeker always lives on the edge, throwing caution to the wind, excitedly jumping in and out of affairs.

Compulsive Affairs

A compulsive individual acts out by engaging in extramarital liaisons over and over. This individual is on an endless, doomed search for the loving mother, the emotional nurturing that was missing in early childhood.

Arrested Development

These individuals are unable to connect with others. They move from one conquest to another in an effort to prove sexual prowess.

A man who engages in this behavior could be called a dog man—a male slut. He may have limited intelligence or, developmentally, still be an adolescent. He proves himself as a 17-year-old does, by hanging sexual conquests on his belt. Generally, individuals displaying arrested development and "dog man" characteristics are men. However, there are also women who shore up self-esteem by wooing and winning a string of men. These individuals feel uncomfortable when others don't know or see their power over the opposite sex.

Bill fits all categories of the philandering male: the male who needs multiple lovers to show off his attractive facade, his sexual prowess and pride in the fact that he is uninterested in attachment.

Bill's need and desire is to pursue the unavailable person. The minute that person gives in to him and becomes a participant in an affair, his attention wanes. He needs another challenge, then he begins another pursuit.

Bill and Barbara

Bill, at 59, called for marriage counseling because his wife of 15 years was divorcing him. Although they had separated several times and tried divorce once, it seemed Barbara was serious this time.

Barbara, Bill's second wife and 17 years his junior, said she was sick of his proclivity for "girls." Elegant, perfectly groomed Barbara began by saying, "Bill is interested in stopping the divorce proceedings. I'm not. I agreed to see you with the idea that I've tried everything. The truth is, I don't believe counseling can save this marriage.

"The reason Bill wants to save the marriage is money. Other than that, he's a dog man. All he does is sniff around and chase other women."

Unable to keep quiet, Bill denied the charge, "The only time I've been involved with other women is when we've been separated."

Barbara snorted and rolled her eyes. Bill continued, "Disregard her opinion, she doesn't know what she's saying."

Thus began their habitual style of interacting. Bill disregarding and denying his wife's allegations, Barbara making ongoing negative comments about Bill.

Barbara said she felt unloved and demeaned by Bill's behavior. Bill responded, "She doesn't mean that."

Barbara was right when she announced counseling could not save her marriage. Flexibility and change are requirements for successful marriage counseling. The second time Bill romanced another woman, it was either time for Barbara to say good-bye or to plan on life with an uncommitted husband, because by then, their lifestyle was established.

Bill and Barbara's marriage counseling was divorce counseling. Barbara's final words, "Better late than never."

Exiting the Relationship

If you suspect your partner is a philandering person, run, don't walk to the nearest exit; unless you want a non-relationship where deceit and humiliation are everyday fare. This partner may admit misdeeds and express contrition, but all the while fingers are crossed behind the back.

Trying to dissuade her/him is like spitting in the wind. Forget change. Forget hope. What you're looking at is what you've got.

Making Relationship Choices

Facts about the philanderer:

> 1. Philanderers have had numbers of other partners, at least one known affair, others suspected.
>
> 2. The philanderer shows lack of commitment, his or her romantic activities are paramount, family tenth on the list.
>
> 3. The philanderer says, "I love only you. S/he means nothing to me. I'm sorry. I'll never do it again." These words mean nothing.
>
> 4. The philanderer acts out every seductive thought.

Your choice is to stay or go. It is important to look at the pattern and take the pattern seriously. If you looked at a kitchen sink you would not expect it to be different in an hour or in a year.

Expect the same with a self-serving person. Habitual style is evidence and predicts future behavior.

Once you understand your partner and the meaning of your partner's affair, you have relationship power. The decisions are yours. However, neither of your choices is a happy one. Staying in the relationship equals unfulfillment, discomfort and pain.

Leaving a marriage is always difficult, complicated and oftentimes torturous. Prepare yourself as best you can with information. Take time to make your decision, then stick to it for at least three months. Recognize you may need even more time than this. Although the urge to do something is strong, quiet yourself. View affair information as a predictor of future behavior. Then answer the question, "Can I tolerate a philanderer's life style?"

CHAPTER 7

WORKING THROUGH A REPAIR AFFAIR

The Repair Affair: An Indirect Fix for the Marriage

A repair affair is meant to fix the marriage and become a means to solve marital difficulties. The repair affair is fueled by situational problems such as low self-esteem, the need for distance or for intimacy. It uses a triangle with an outside person to shock the marital system into change.

Your marriage has its own contract. While that contract may not be articulated, it is understood by you and your spouse. Unwritten marital contracts cover interacting, physical and emotional care-taking.

Sex is part of that contract. It's understood married people have sex, but often individual expectations differ. You may expect sex once a week, your wife or husband may believe sex should be a daily event. You see the difficulty you're in? Particularly because no words have been exchanged to determine a "sex schedule."

When your marriage contract is broken, your relationship is in trouble. There are periods when you cannot fulfill one or more of your partner's needs, and at times there may be shifts in what is needed and expected in the marriage. For example, one partner may need physical contact several times daily to feel attended to and loved. If, for some reason, the other spouse is unavailable--mentally absorbed elsewhere or physically

The Repair Affair

inaccessible, and can't or won't respond to his or her partner's needs--the contract is broken.

Understanding the "Whys" of a Repair Affair

A partner may begin a repair affair when the spouse is absorbed in a job, a baby, parents, something or someone other than the partner. When self esteem is at low ebb, and the partner feels abandoned, h/she may look for attention and respect through an affair. Often one partner feels genuinely deprived. For example, the man believes he is the "wallet" (material things are of primary value); the woman feels she is the "housekeeper."

Sex is often an affair prompter, particularly for a male. However, women are also susceptible. Some of the reasons an individual seeks sexual fulfillment outside the marriage include:

- Quantity and quality of sex required is missing.

- Situational issues inhibit sexual desire: physically exhausting jobs, different shifts, unemployment, presence of preschool children.

- Problems that result from long-term management of a physically ill or psychologically disturbed child or parent.

- Opportunity presents itself in a situation away from home, often alcohol is involved.

At this moment in time the partner feels helpless, hopeless and unable to solve the marital problem or express dissatisfaction in ways which get the other partner's attention. The dissatisfied partner may:

- Expect that the spouse will magically see and understand

- Neither understand nor express distress

- Express difficulty only to have the partner dismiss the words, not comprehend the depth of unhappiness, or not really hear what's being said.

Tina's dilemma was that she loved Gregg and wanted a happy marriage, but the overwhelming demands of her life obliterated Gregg's needs. Tina focused on Gregg as the source of the problem when her marriage blew up.

Tina and Gregg
Her dark hair pulled back casually, Tina, 39, is an automotive engineer, gaunt and almost anorexic, with sad, large brown eyes. Poised, she stood as stiff as a board, deliberately keeping herself under control.

Tina worked full time, was going to school and also took care of the house and children with Gregg's sporadic help. The pace of her life was frantic; she understood Gregg was needy and unhappy with his career, but she figured he would get over it, as she herself had done in many similar situations.

She had neither the time nor energy to see Gregg's problem. Gregg's self-esteem was at an all-time low, and he desperately sought comfort from his wife.

Tina denied the possibility of her husband's involvement with another woman until she could no longer discount the evidence. Her husband and another woman? Impossible, she

The Repair Affair

and Gregg were too close. Clues pointing to an affair stirred disbelief. Finally the evidence was overwhelming.

In the past when Tina saw Gregg and her best friend, Roslyn, together she felt uncomfortable and slightly jealous. But she dismissed the feelings, and got mad at herself for being so "small-minded and foolish."

Gregg had recently told Tina he was involved with Roslyn, but only after he was confronted with facts. Although Tina suspected an affair, when she confronted Gregg and he confessed, she was in shock.

At her first therapy session Tina began speaking before she sat down, "I have these periods when I feel like screaming. I just can't stand what is going on. Today is one of those times. My skin feels too tight.

"I'm so relieved to have set up this appointment, I can't contain myself. I have a problem I can't discuss with anyone. My husband has been having an affair with my best friend for more than a year." Tina's eyes watered, then she began to cry, "I'm sorry."

For several minutes she fought for control, then continued, "I'm O.K. now. This is what I do at home and in the car. One minute I'm sobbing, can't think straight, the next I can think calmly and rationally. I definitely don't feel normal. I'm consumed by Gregg's affair; it's all I think about. How could he have done this to us and especially with one of my best friends. I think about humiliating Roslyn in front of her family, murdering her, torturing her, burning a big red "A" on her forehead.

"At the same time I'm paralyzed with fear that Gregg and Roslyn will ride off into a love sunset. Even though Gregg has said it was over and he's sorry, it's as if my brain doesn't comprehend. It doesn't compute. I fear Gregg is setting up a ploy to keep fooling me and maintain the status quo for himself and Roslyn.

"At night I fall asleep after hours of tortured thoughts. Then, just as quickly I wake up, my brain immediately snaps into the affair."

Tina swallowed a sob, "More and more in the past year I felt something was happening to Gregg or to us. I thought he was acting strange. I couldn't quite put my finger on what was different about him but I never put the bits and pieces together. Maybe I didn't want to. When I think back, I was a sap! An attraction between Gregg and Roslyn was inconceivable to me. Roslyn is not attractive. She's dumpy and dopey, but lovable in her way. I guess I thought she was only lovable to another woman.

"Before I discovered the affair Gregg and I talked about my perception that he had changed. We've always been open with one another. You must think that's a joke. Put it this way, I was open. Gregg said he didn't have the answer, he didn't think he was different."

Tina said she had been vaguely unhappy for a long time, like something was wrong. She submerged those thoughts and feelings: "It was probably me; I tend to be a perfectionist. I considered the possibility of Gregg having an affair but discarded that thought because I almost always knew where he was." Tina blamed her hormones, her job, her kids, her overload at home and at work.

"I ended up without an answer, feeling like a dope because I had everything--nice husband and kids, beautiful home and satisfying job. I began to think I was simply a person who had to find something to crab about. Gregg reinforced this attitude, saying, 'You always find something to bitch about.' That statement puts me in a rage now, because I believed him! He knew what he was up to, and he had the balls to turn on me."

It took a year of uneasiness and denying reality before Tina took herself seriously. Yes, Gregg was different. Yes, clues led somewhere. Yes, something was wrong, but it wasn't within Tina. It was outside of her. Tina discovered Gregg's affair "accidentally."

One Friday Gregg used their 16-year-old son's car, and dropped Tina off at Roslyn's for a bridge party, saying he would come back later. When Tina put her hors d'oeuvre in the back seat, she picked up a barrette on the floor. When she showed Gregg the barrette, he claimed he'd never seen it before. Tina realized she had. It was Roslyn's.

This was the second time an article of Roslyn's had turned up in one of their cars. Tina's heart began to pound and her breast heaved. Her face felt flushed as her mind rushed back in time.

Roslyn had always been a favorite of Gregg's. Roslyn and Gregg talked together for long periods of time at neighborhood social functions. When their group of friends went up North, Tina often took the kids early, leaving Gregg and Roslyn to drive together. Sometimes

Randy, Roslyn's husband, accompanied them; sometimes they drove alone.

At Roslyn's house Tina got out of the car and went in, the hors d'oeuvres forgotten. Tonight was the first of many great performances, a series of tortuous hours when Tina felt anguished and sick inside, but presented her normal self to her friends.

Tina continued, "At times I think my life is over. Facing Gregg's infidelity is terrible. I'm the one suffering; he isn't. I can't sleep. I cry on and off every day. I keep asking him why and what happened. I'm madder than hell one minute and fearful he'll leave the next. I keep him up at night or wake him up to ask questions or vent my anger. I talk through clenched teeth and feel I want to kill.

"In my heart I wonder if their relationship continues. I imagine Gregg secretly talking to her, plotting a meeting. I know where he is every minute now so a rendezvous between them is unlikely. Still, that fear is real.

"Gregg is trying to listen to me. Whenever I want to talk, and it's always about the affair, he puts down whatever he's doing and pays attention to me. I even get up in the middle of the night. I wake up like a bolt, my mind in gear, thinking of an aspect of the affair that I overlooked or think I overlooked.

"Naturally the kids are asking what's wrong. I'm not involving them, but I did talk to my neighbor, Joanie. And she was shocked. She's a good friend of Roslyn's, too, and knows what a flake she is.

"I have this overwhelming urge to talk to Roslyn, confront her, put her down, find out

The Repair Affair

what in the world she thought she was doing." Tina leaned toward me, "What do you think? Would it help the situation? Gregg is scared to death I'll create more of a stir. Maybe Gregg should come in and talk to you."

We agreed Gregg's participation in therapy would be helpful. Tina would ask him, and if he agreed, he would call for an appointment.

When Tina and I met again, her husband had not called. Tina began the session stating, "Gregg said he can't stand the continual questioning and crying, but I can't stop. I told Gregg what you said, that it would be a good idea for him to talk to you. But as far as he's concerned, the affair is over and there's nothing to talk about. If I want, he will come in but I think he's afraid. I know he'd be nervous. He's always said he can't understand why people have to see psychologists."

After Tina and I met for several more sessions, Gregg called and made an appointment as an "aid to Tina's therapy."

Gregg, 44, knocked timidly on the door to announce his arrival. When I opened the door I was surprised as he walked in, introduced himself and proceeded to remove a wide brimmed hat and an overly long, but expensive looking overcoat. He was short, stocky, with thick hair, an on-the-shoulder curly mane, beard and mustache, a silk shirt and pleated pants. He resembled an off-Broadway production.

I expected a Shakespearean quote. Instead, he spoke softly and gently, "You know our situation, so I won't go over the details. There are undoubtedly questions you'd like me to answer, please feel free to ask anything."

Before I had a chance to say anything Gregg said, "I desperately want the marriage. I love Tina and want to keep her. I'm here because Tina is having such a hard time getting over her hurt and anger. I tell her daily I'm sorry about the whole thing. I tell her I love her and have no intention of ever seeing Roslyn again. It calms her for a minute, but then she starts again. I need help from you to know what to do or what to say."

Gregg called the affair "accidental." He said he was sorry and wanted to get on with life. The affair, Gregg explained, had to do with the state of his ego rather than proof that love had disintegrated or was gone from the marriage.

Gregg's business had recently failed, and he was reduced to a sales job he detested. At the same time, Tina was absorbed in work and school as she completed her master's degree in engineering.

Gregg's father was a known womanizer, and as Gregg grew up he and his siblings knew father was out and about. Since in Gregg's family there were no known repercussions for infidelity, we might say an affair was accepted behavior. Gregg's father was his model.

Gregg presented himself as sorry about the painful consequences for Tina. In fact, he was surprised by Tina's profound reaction. His affair was a compensatory, albeit unconscious, move by Gregg to rivet Tina's attention on him. Consciously, it backfired as negative energy, lack of trust; disgust and fear became daily fare in his marriage. Unconsciously his affair worked: Tina's being was focused totally on Gregg.

Gregg's ego was elevated, Tina's ego was crushed. The trauma of her husband's involvement with Roslyn became a temporary loss of her "self." She viewed herself as a failure: a woman rejected and socially humiliated, her family destroyed and her self-respect gone. Trust and innocence were gone for Tina; she would never be the same.

Rubbing the Slate Clean After a Repair Affair

The question is, how can an affair like Gregg's repair a marriage?

An affair alerts partners that loss of the relationship is possible. Powerful motivation to be together can refocus and force real communication. Early marital tender loving care can be reinstituted with desire.

In relationships people become sloppy in their treatment of each other; disregarding, demanding, disrespecting, treating partners unlike the friends they were during courtship. Too often, partners act as though a good relationship is their birthright. They become angry if things don't go their way. Their attitude is "my way is the only way."

If your mate tells you s/he's had an affair, then what? Will you accept the admission and be happy s/he's an honest person and really trying to maintain the marriage? **No Way.** The admission steam-rolls into your mind and turns on a switch you didn't know you had, splattering and fragmenting thoughts and emotions.

One can be committed in a marriage, as Gregg is, and yet behave as if the relationship is of no value by having an affair. People seldom think of the consequences before deciding, "Yes, I believe I will have an affair." The thoughts, "This is wrong. No, I don't want to do it but I can't help myself," may salve the conscience. But they also begin a string of rationalizations underpinned by the concept, "I want what I want when I want it."

Surviving Affair Aftershock

Affairs elevate the self esteem of the infidel. Affairs crush the self esteem of the betrayed.

What exactly *is* self esteem? Self esteem is what you think and feel about yourself, your experience, your confidence in yourself.

The unfaithful partner uses the affair as an alter ego elevator (the alter ego is outside our selves rather than within) to ward off plummeting confidence and to fill the mind. An affair changes a person's state. An affair might divert and excite the mind, temporarily restoring a confident state to replace the battered and bruised feelings that no amount of solace from self or normal supports has been able to help.

As the betrayed, an affair dramatically changes your confidence in the world. It's no longer a safe place. Worse, plummeting self esteem tells you aren't lovable, you've failed. Trust in yourself and your partner disappears. Your self esteem is gone.

Discovery of an affair shatters partnership trust, which is the bottom line in a relationship. Once trust is cracked, it can be healed. But welding and integrating the wound so that the mind is soothed and calmed takes a long time. The scar never disappears. Years after the affair, old nasty feelings fall back into the heart with a jolt. Once you are betrayed, some part of you will forever more be vigilant.

Tina struggled with trust but was determined, along with Gregg, that their marriage was viable. The repair worked as they gained understanding of the purpose of the affair and how and why it occurred. Their goal was satisfaction, excitement and contentment. In other words a better marriage with focused, positive time together. If a week looked as if it was going to be hectic, Tina and Gregg set up time to be together just as they would allocate time for a business appointment. They learned to express feelings safely and focused on respecting one another (listening and allowing the other safe expression of thoughts and feelings). They continually kept in mind their goal: marital commitment and satisfaction.

The saying, "It's never over till it's over," is true of affairs. Gregg and Tina very quickly found there were complications they had not anticipated as a result of his affair.

Tina called for a consultation. When they came in, Tina insisted Gregg do the talking:

Gregg said, "Life has been relatively quiet since Tina's feeling better and beginning to trust me. I'm feeling my family is not going to fall apart, but I recently had an incident that is making me paranoid.

"I was out jogging and Roslyn's husband, Rod, pulled up next to me in his car and said he wanted to talk to me. I felt like I was being attacked by a cobra, but I agreed to talk with him. He said he'd come over in a couple of hours and would like Tina to be there, too. The next two hours were like slow motion for me. I imagined every possible scenario and felt very nervous. When he arrived he wouldn't come into the house.

"He stood outside and said he knew everything and simply wanted to talk man to man with me. I couldn't help thinking, if that was true, why did he want Tina present? Anyway, he

started talking, 'Who did I think I was' and 'What was I doing with his wife.' His voice escalated and I was afraid the whole neighborhood could hear so I told him to come inside. He wouldn't. Finally I said, 'We're (meaning Tina and I) going inside.' Well, he kind of grabbed at me and Tina lunged at him and we did an embarrassing mini-wrestling scene on the lawn. Tina said, 'Stop it." Rod left with the warning, "This is not over."

Affairs profoundly affect the nature of relationships and often have unexpected consequences. As it turned out there were no further incidents with Roslyn's husband, but Gregg's tussle with Rod so frightened both Gregg and Tina they decided their once friendly, comfortable neighborhood was no longer a safe haven. They moved out of town.

Relationship Distance

I'll end this chapter with a brief look at four other kinds of relationships that can spark repair affairs, each characterized by distance of some type.

Distant Marriage/Can't Let Go

This affair avoids issues and maintains distance while keeping the marriage intact. The individual having the affair is able to stay in the marriage because of the diversion the affair provides. Partners in a distant marriage never argue. They avoid conflict regardless of the cost. They appear rational and are apparently happy with one another. Feelings, resentment, disapproval or disappointment, are not acknowledged. The partner most dissatisfied shatters the facade of amiability and perfection by having an affair.

The Repair Affair

The basic motive for this type of affair is to bring attention to marital difficulties and repair the relationship. Relationship repair does not occur if the affair is not acknowledged. Ignorance of an affair means partners don't have to recognize problems or take action. The affair limits intimacy and closeness. When the uninvolved spouse realizes something's wrong but the partner denies and the denial is accepted, the affair aids distance.

Constant Conflict

The opposite of the relationship above is found in partners who can't communicate or are constantly hostile or arguing. To ward off intimacy, they establish a style of constant conflict. An affair provides relief from the conflict in such a relationship.

When the affair is discovered by the other partner, it leads to more arguing and provides the fuel for a lifetime of anger and resentment.

On the other hand, the crisis brought about by the discovery of an affair may catapult partners into growth and a new marital style.

Workaholic

The workaholic may be using the affair and its discovery to force behavioral change. This individual may not be aware of emotions or may live for work, finding emotions a problem or a bother. The spouse now has leverage to force changes in the marital system and has an opportunity to look within her/himself.

Authoritarian/Dependent

The original, although unwritten, marriage contract often places husband in the role of provider, head of the house and final authority on all matters. As partners mature there is a shift in roles.

The dominant person gives up some power and the dependent person takes charge and/or takes over in designated areas of the relationship.

If one partner needs change while the other is rooted to the spot and does not give or at least bend, either by becoming interdependent or relinquishing authority, an affair can change the equation as it did in the case of Tracy and George.

Tracy and George

Married 29 years, Tracy looked extraordinarily young; in fact, I rechecked the year she was born. Tracy's hair was pulled back in a pony tail, her face unlined.

Tracy said her husband, George, insisted she was having an affair with an old high school classmate. He said he could tell by the way they talked together at their class reunion eight years ago. It looked to George as if they were arguing. "You only argue with people you are intimate with," he insisted.

Tracy told George she had never entertained the idea of an affair, but George couldn't give it up. Always suspicious and on guard, George's theme throughout the marriage was to keep others out, all others, including Tracy's family. He wanted Tracy in lock-step with him.

Although Tracy was a world-champion pleaser and her husband was at the head of her list of people to please, she eventually felt stifled and unable to be herself.

Tracy became self-conscious about her every move, worried George would think she was

The Repair Affair

at the store too long, was looking at a male seductively or was not conducting herself properly by George's standards.

George did not want Tracy out and about but, by squashing her initiative, George shot himself in the foot. He either couldn't or simply didn't try to understand his jealousy and distrust.

Well, guess what? Tracy wasn't involved in an affair eight years ago. But she is now and has been for five months. George's suppression of Tracy, his insistence on togetherness to the exclusion of all others and his accusatory style was too much for her.

George became suspicious when Tracy began receiving more phone calls than usual. First curious, then suspicious, George rushed to answer every call. He intercepted a phone call from Tracy's lover. When George confronted Tracy, she immediately confessed, said she was sorry, loved George and wanted the marriage.

George went into shock; his accusations were part of Tracy control. He wasn't prepared for reality. For a time he needed anti-depressants and sleeping medication to settle down, to be in the world and to change thinking patterns.

The marriage has survived and both Tracy and George report higher marital satisfaction. The affair began a major overhaul of the marriage, a circuitous and unfortunate method to repair the marriage.

Recognizing Indicators of a Repair Affair

Here's how to tell if your mate's affair is meant to repair your relationship:

1. When confronted with affair information, your spouse immediately confesses and reports being sorry.

2. Your partner allows your pain, is understanding, and does his or her best to listen and answer questions.

3. Your partner reiterates his or her love and desire for the relationship, not just for two weeks or a month, rather, indefinitely.

Repair affairs can shock and change your marital system positively. Once the affair trauma subsides, there is the possibility of a dramatic relationship change. Repair affairs are opportunities for expanding, improving and developing relationships.

Bridge affairs, on the other hand, lead you out of the relationship, into a new life with new adventures. Self-serving affairs provide information about your spouse's character.

Once the purpose of your spouse's affair is clear, the decision is yours. Your job is to decide whether you want to proceed with or without your partner.

SECTION THREE

RECREATING YOURSELF

CHAPTER EIGHT

LEAVING THE PAST AND ENTERING THE FUTURE WITH OR WITHOUT YOUR PARTNER

Recreating and Bringing Order to Your World With Your Partner

You have survived the most shocking stages of the betrayal. But your journey is far from over. Now you face decisions that will lead to pain or to growth.

This is crunch time. Will you leave your pain behind and use the affair for growth, or will the affair subdue your spirit permanently?

When the press revealed in August 1996, that President Clinton's campaign adviser, Dick Morris, had, not only consorted with a prostitute on a regular basis, but had a long term affair with another woman (with whom he had a child), his wife's first public reaction was to stay by his side. Eileen McGann searched her soul for six months, then decided the relentless publicity and other considerations made it imperative for her to file for divorce.

Eileen McGann's painful journey began with the intention of saving the marriage. She then declared the marriage over. Recently I noticed a newspaper article stating they are back together!

Each of us who faces the devastation of an affair has similar, difficult choices--to remain together or part.

Recognizing Your Choices

Once you have absorbed the emotional impact and grasped the consequences of your partner's affair, how do you begin to make choices about your relationship? You have options:

- You choose.
- H/she chooses.
- It's a joint decision.
- Life chooses for you.

Ideally, you make the decision; life **with** or **without** her/him. Even if s/he opts to leave, you still have options pertaining to your new role in life.

Following discovery of an affair, some people do not recover. They are scarred for life and remain miserable. Since you don't want to feel distraught, upset, angry and revengeful for the rest of your life, or even for the rest of today, the question is, "What do you want?"

Your ideas need to be reasonable. It is not reasonable to think/dream, "I want life the way it used to be." Life is not going to be as it used to be. More than that, you wouldn't want to have to go through the affair anguish again.

When you opt for misery, you keep the affair alive in your mind and preoccupy your family and allies with your misery.

Other poor choices are: Allowing your spouse to call the shots and accept whatever s/he chooses to deal out to you; go into your shell; never talk about the affair; ignore the affair. Or, hide out in your marriage, fearfully remaining in a one-dimensional role as wife-woman or husband/money/maker. Frightened your spouse will leave, you cave in and become a slave. Another option is to make up and have essentially the same pre-affair relationship, without losing or gaining much.

Let's face it, you've been slam-dunked into hell, rejected and humiliated by your spouse, the fact is, you can choose to:

- Struggle against the realities of being rejected.
- Become the helpless victim and go to pieces.
- Acknowledge reality and reconstruct your life.

Between the fateful intuitive moment or factual moment you knew your spouse was unfaithful and this moment, you have become a profoundly different person. When you view yourself as wiser and stronger, rather than a victim, you are propelled forward. Status quo is not satisfactory.

Analyzing Solutions

In both repair affairs and self-serving affairs your spouse wants to maintain the marriage, wants you and is sorry. A bridge affair seldom turns into a walk-about where a U-turn brings your mate back home.

More important, if your partner does walk back into your life, will s/he stay and do you really want this person? You may enjoy the respite of your mate's return; it salves the ego and provides momentary stabilization, but the feeling is momentary. Emotional detachment is permanent after a bridge affair.

On the other hand, you are in the driver's seat when you recognize whether your partner is a philanderer or whether the affair was meant to repair the relationship. Repair affairs and ego-inflating affairs provide options. This is the relationship junction where you determine whether or not you want the relationship.

If you've decided to divorce, move on to Chapter 9.

Choosing Growth

If you choose growth, mentally stay in the present. You must at this decisive moment take charge of your mind and stop obsessing over affair details: why, when, how, where. Affair facts eventually will be integrated into the history of your life. In the meantime, aid your recovery by making decisions about what you want for yourself.

Change your self. First, let go of the past and forgive your partner--as best you can--and, secondly, change your relationship interactions and behaviors.

Taking Action

Stumbling along, figuring out how to proceed by yourself is one solution. But I have found that individuals who move ahead with the least trauma, who find their way out of despair in or out of the marriage, follow particular steps.

At this time it may seem impossible but, yes, you can do it--one step at a time.

There are two major facets of action in this method:

- Manage your thoughts, feelings and behavior
- Reconstruct the relationship

Concrete self-improvement plans, like keeping a diary or exercising, are parts of your life that can be seen and understood.

Recognizing mental habits and self-talk are trickier areas since you have to take a new look at established habits of thinking.

We give our thoughts credence whether it's deserved or not, and we usually accept without exception what comes to mind. The whirrings of your mind direct your life and explain your consciousness to you.

These historical, habitual thoughts may not be relevant or helpful to you at this point in your life, since they are old habits and reactions. Instead of following those old habits and reactions, try this plan:

- Make changes by following Part I: Manage your thoughts, feelings and behavior.

- Continue onward with Part II: Create an extraordinary relationship.

Part I: Managing Thoughts, Feelings, and Behavior

Step One: *Thoughts and Interior Dialogue*

You are the catalyst. You speed your mental health process by refocused attention. Your mind may seem to have a life of its own but thoughts can be directed and redirected. Direct your mind and replace historical, affair focused, upsetting inner dialogue with concrete, positive, future-oriented ideas.

You believe at times you can't help what your mind does. And there are times when your mind is in chaos. Your mind takes charge and obsessively goes over and over what your partner has said and done. Why did s/he do this to me? Why didn't I notice? What's wrong with me?

Did this thinking help? **No.** Does it make you miserable? **Yes**. You need to control your mind. When you begin to practice controlling your thoughts, you may be in control just seconds. However, like any training, time, patience and focus produce results. You are the mind-master.

You've already noticed you have moments, maybe even an hour, when your mind is at peace. In those moments you've closed the door to the past. Now is the time to open the door to new ideas.

In other words, place new words and dialogue of hopefulness and positive possibilities where thoughts and feelings of despair, depression and anxiety grew. Your job, if you desire happiness and peace of mind, is to present new dialogue to your mind.

For example, you are startled by a graphic picture or a sudden thought related to the affair and you automatically fill in the picture. Your mind gasps with pain. You fall back into feelings of rage with negative, historical dialogue cascading into your waiting brain cells.

The second you realize what you are doing, tell yourself "Stop!" Then keep saying stop until your mind is clear, and negative dialogue and feelings are gone. Thoughts generate feelings; negative thoughts generate negative feelings.

You can't help thoughts from coming into your mind, but you can decide what to do with them once they surface. You are not going to solve the affair problem by going over it again and again, nor are you going to feel good by reliving your pain.

So, if that's where your mind is, **STOP IT RIGHT NOW**.

And don't whine that these thoughts keep coming back without your control. Of course they keep coming back. You've established a powerful habit. Expect these thoughts to fill your mind.

Rather, dramatically focus your attention on the present, keep on track in the present moment. Let those confusing, angry and fearful thoughts go.

When an affair thought floats into your mind, move it out and replace it with a positive thought or wrap the thought up in a garbage bag and give it a violent heave-ho.

Your job is to accept reality, recognize the thought as simply a thought, let go and forgive. Forgive by reminding yourself you are not the judge and jury of yourself or your spouse.

It's not your job to blame and determine the whys of the affair. It happened. It's a fact. Let it go.

Keep working at it. Practice makes perfect.

Step Two: *Manage Your Emotions*

Initially the shock of the affair takes over and for a period of time feelings run rampant. However, those feelings gradually subside, and you will realize you do have feeling choices. By consciously paying attention to intruding, destructive thoughts, you determine their path. You can foster them or move them out of your mind. Your emotions are under your control.

You may be unaware you have an ongoing dialogue in your mind, a dialogue that runs rampant and directs feelings. At the least, thoughts about the affair will distress your emotional system. Count on it. In the worst case, your thoughts stir up feelings that are overwhelming. These overwhelming thoughts alarm your system and trigger urgent messages to the brain. Your heart races; your blood pressure rises; your facial expressions become distressed and your fight or flight hormones are triggered.

If emotions overwhelm and take control of you, you are their victim. When you are so sensitive to emotion that it amounts to an affliction, it eliminates your ability to reason. You are addicted and controlled by your emotional/limbic system. In this case I openly and specifically recommend medical psychiatric intervention and therapy to interrupt the clutch of these feelings.

You have options. Your intellectual life and emotional life should dance in harmony: Emotion is the music; inner dialogue is the emotion conductor.

Step Three: *Sabotage and Retraining*

You live in your mind. Do not fill it with poison. Thoughts that sabotage growth and development are poison. You can easily sabotage positive thoughts with what seems to be reality. For example, "I'd like to attend Imago Relationship classes but...I can't. I don't have money or time. I can't concentrate. My emotions are out of control." Wrong! You can do anything.

Negative thoughts--no money, no time, no concentration, wild emotions--are tricks you've developed to sabotage yourself and be inactive. These tricks protect you for that moment. But this kind of fantasy, which you view as reality, is the baby in you being defensive.

Your brain is a computer. It accepts input as real. That's why you feel anxious and/or depressed long after the affair. The affair triggers primitive fears of insecurity. Those fear thoughts still generate emotions, feel real, fill your mind and inhibit action.

You sabotage your own thoughts in many ways. For example, if you have decided to try to remain in the relationship, you find yourself thinking, "I love Jim." Then frightening ideas come to mind: "Maybe he doesn't love me; maybe he's continuing his affair; maybe he's pretending to want the marriage." These are natural thoughts.

But your job is to stay with the idea that you love Jim and that you want the marriage. This is your decision, your goal, and you must struggle to remain in-tune and focused.

I know sometimes it's easier to slump back into depression or into old thoughts and behaviors rather than force yourself to take charge and stay targeted on the goal.

Do not sabotage your mind plan. Rather, deliberately and slowly tell yourself that you are in charge. You are beginning a new inner life. **PAY ATTENTION** to your mental dialogue.

Step Four: *Incorporate Five Behaviors Into Your Daily Rhythm*

1. Take time out
2. Plan
3. Write
4. Exercise
5. Meditate

Take Time Out

If you hear distressing mental dialogue, say to yourself either, "Stop or Enough!" Then mentally move into a different space or, if possible, physically change your affect, which means take action, remove yourself. **Train your concentration to respond: "Enough."**

Plan

When you get into bed at night set a plan for the next day, beginning when you awaken. You will then have an immediate morning schedule established for both physical and mental behavior minute by minute.

Write

Carry a small notebook and jot down your ideas as they occur. Keep a daily journal of your thoughts and feelings. Write in it the first thing in the morning and the last thing at night. This will help you note the times of day or night when negative patterns occur and prepare you to combat those down times.

If you awaken during the night immediately turn on the light and write about thoughts and feelings, dreams, and/or positive future plans. Don't let yourself ruminate, slip into the past and begin a self-defeating, mood-altering, downward spiral.

Exercise

Exercise on and off all day. If possible exercise one hour a day. You can exercise in five minute sets. Carry a jump rope to work, run in place or walk around the building. You need physical release of tension.

Meditate

Meditation is a method to access your inner life, to think deeply and continuously, bypassing your conscious mind. If you don't already know how, buy a book which gives step-by-step details of how to meditate. The point you're aiming at with these four behaviors is taking control and managing yourself.

Time is your ally. The more time between the affair and the present, the better you will feel. In the meantime and hopefully forever more, take care of yourself with healthy mental and physical behavior. **You will feel better.**

Step Five: *Use Therapy to Educate Yourself*

If the past keeps getting in the way, choose a therapist

and work through the past.

Dealing with the past helps you understand the connection between today's behavior and thoughts and historical learning, environment, relationship interactions and your personality. Therapy needn't be devoted to the past, but links to the past will illuminate the present.

Use therapy to educate yourself. Like it or not, you cannot be objective about yourself. A therapist will give you useful information both about yourself and your relationship. Therapy speeds the healing process and may catapult you quickly into a change mode.

These five steps in managing your thoughts, feelings and behavior are personal accomplishments, methods to develop the life you want in a thoughtful, positive way.

Your mind has been running rampant, with good reason. Affair trauma produces chaos everywhere in life: in your relationships, within your self, and in your environment.

Part Two: Creating an Extraordinary Relationship

The rhythm of your life has altered dramatically and you are in the process of what is called a "paradigm shift." You are shifting into the unknown. The present is a shambles and the future unknowable. All you have is this moment in time; all that is knowable is where you are now.

This is your opportunity to dynamite routine patterns! Old methods of being together didn't work.

Good! You understand now what wasn't successful, so consider yourself in an experimental stage, jump-starting and rewiring your couple connection.

To give your relationship every chance of success you need to be aware of all the ways you communicate, including negative habits. It's important to dedicate yourselves to developing intimate, open communications including listening skills and self expression.

Habitual Communication

Good communication is vital for friendship and intimacy. Changing habitual communication patterns takes time and perseverance. Since we are not objective about our own communication styles, you may unwittingly perpetuate styles you don't want.

Watch out for habits that communicate:

- As the innocent person your position is right, s/he is wrong.

- You blame your partner; s/he's at fault.

- You're the innocent victim, the martyr.

- You deny feelings. (No, you aren't sad, angry, hurt; everything's rosy.)

- You blame yourself, acting as if you are at fault.

- Your tone is cutting, sarcastic or hostile.

- You are defensive, immediately explaining or denying, fighting fire with fire, rather than being empathic or simply listening.

- You use the silent treatment, with-draw and pout.

- You bring up past injustices.

The tension from an affair magnifies any past communication method. You developed and probably perfected your magical thinking as you strained to read between the lines of secrets and affair lies. Magical thinking means you imagine what s/he's thinking, or you interpret words and behavior, taking your ideas as the truth without clarification.

When you're together and angry thoughts arise--and they will--don't be a party to them. In other words, you catch the gist of your feeling and the beginning mental dialogue, "How could s/he have done that? That makes me so mad!" Instead, insert other calming words. "I'm so happy we're together and building a new relationship. I feel good."

Replace negative thoughts with any uplifting, energetic, positive thoughts that shift you into this present moment and advance your goal for relationship peace and pleasure.

Good communication means you express feelings openly and directly and encourage your partner's expression of feelings. You listen and try to understand what his or her thoughts and feelings involve.

When trouble looms, the smartest move you can make is to look within yourself and at your own communication style immediately, exploring changes you can make.

Jac's marital difficulties were compounded by lack of communication skills. Fortunately, Jac was insight oriented and open to change.

Jac and Judy

Jac, 43, a junior college instructor, and I had established a trusting therapeutic relationship through months of his marital trauma. Today Jac looked as he had the first day we met, clothes disheveled, rubbing his eyes and pushing his hands through his hair.

Jac said, "This situation is complicated, it has a lot of parts. You know me, I'm a Youper (from the Upper Peninsula of Michigan) and I don't know if my perceptions are correct. I've been praying Judy would return and be herself. Now her 'self' is back."

Jac stared at me as if to divine magically my reaction, "Judy confessed." She said, 'I'm sorry; I'm so sorry. He meant nothing. I love you. I do not want a divorce.' These are the exact words I had been waiting to hear, but now I'm scared. I don't know her."

Desperately trying to get his relationship with Judy back on track, Jac had come into therapy at his sister's suggestion. According to Jac, when Judy, 36, a part-time medical transcriptionist, began college two years ago, their marriage disintegrated. Jac, to his credit, took full responsibility for Judy's unhappiness, explaining that, from the beginning of the marriage, he left Judy alone five or six nights a week while he participated in sports. His rationale at that time was, "I told her when we married that I needed sports and wouldn't give them up.

"I never really changed my style. Being a Youper, I guess you could say I'm not sophisticated and my confidence totally had to do with sports. I'm good, I'd even say excellent, at any sport I try. But, as it turns out, sports ruined my marriage. Maybe, not being a talker was also a problem. Another big issue in Judy's mind, is that I like to make people laugh. When we're out, I'm a joker. Judy calls me a clown, which I guess means I'm really not funny, probably a fool.

"So, I know why Judy's sick of me. Judy says I haven't been her companion, and I agree. I haven't helped with the children. I'm trying to catch up now which doesn't cut it with her. But I can't stop trying to get her back, trying to get her to love me. At least I want her to tell me everything's all right with the marriage. I can hear myself and know I need to shut up, but I can't. She's so angry with me all the time, I can't stand it. And on top of everything, I'm worried about the other man."

Making a Dramatic Change

Going from one extreme to another, Jac replaced his sports obsession with wife obsession. In therapy Jac finally calmed down and decided to interact differently with Judy, respect her, focus on her and knock off the interrogations.

Jac also cut down his participation in sports, sometimes not playing at all or playing only once a week. This turned out to be too much togetherness for Judy. Although she had complained of his absence, she began to encourage him to bowl or golf or at least occasionally get out.

Jac was also trying to be affectionate and not just sexual, which was difficult for him, since his family of origin was rigid in every way. In fact, Jac cannot remember a time when his father or mother talked with or to him.

Still, as a teacher Jac talked; learning was his forte. But Jac said he felt uncomfortable and awkward when he attempted personal, intimate communication.

It was time to decide. Was Jac willing to work through his resistance to intimacy and could he tolerate

Judy's infidelity? "I love her, I want her. That's the bottom line," Jac declared, looking frantically at me, at the same time nervously moving his hands around his face. "But I don't want the marriage we had, and I don't want the marriage my parents had. That means starting over."

As Jac took control of himself, backed off, and allowed Judy room to breathe, the relationship slowly improved.

Fortunately Jac had nothing to lose and everything to gain. Critical factors in successful reuniting are desire, motivation and knowledge. Negative thoughts and feelings will enter Jac's mind and take over, as will ideas that Judy "should" act in a certain way or say particular things. Trust will be a major factor as time passes. Jac has been instructed to:

- Eliminate responses that are argumentative, oppositional or defensive.
- Acknowledge and express feelings openly and directly.
- Acknowledge his wife's feelings.
- Respect Judy by taking her words seriously.

The marriage is better than it has ever been. Problems for Jac arise when anger and fear fill his mind. Constant verbalizations of distress soon become harassment but, since Jac tends to be stoic, he has been taught in therapy to focus on expressing himself, and trust Judy to tell him if she feels overwhelmed.

Jac and Judy have made great strides and have dramatically changed their dull, unaffectionate and, at times, nasty union to one where they are having fun, being affectionate and sexual, and communicating openly.

Reassurances

Chances are you will need intermittent help from your spouse while you are resuming your connection as a couple.

On a daily basis, for **six months to a year,** let your mate know that you will need reassurance that:

- S/he loves you.
- The other person is gone and your partner is interested only in you.
- S/he will never stray again.
- S/he understands at least some of your pain.

At the same time, reassurances are often an annoyance to your spouse because s/he wants you to "get over it." Reassurances also are a reminder of guilt, something your spouse would like to forget.

So, be nice, don't beat your partner with your sorrow, your disappointment, your hurt. When your mind is obsessed with questions, cool it.

Interrogations don't work well. Rather, they keep you both stuck in the past. Your purpose isn't to grind your partner down, it's to soothe and calm yourself while establishing new parameters for your relationship.

Privacy

Reassurance dialogues are intimate, emotional and necessary while you rework your partnership.

Let your mate know that hearing those words are a necessity to you. But, don't drag the talks out even if you'd like to be steeped in reassurances every minute. Set a time frame and stick to it.

If you didn't pick up on the affair right away, you may feel socially or personally embarrassed. You may feel as if every friend and acquaintance knew of his or her indiscretion, and you didn't. Or you may feel you weren't tuned in, so you feel stupid and take responsibility.

The truth is, it is embarrassing and stupefying because we expect ourselves to pick up any nuance with our partner. We forget that part of the partner's affair-job was distortion and disguise.

A cardinal rule in most relationships is to keep private lives private. Never go public. You may feel that your private life is public and, even if others don't know, it may feel as if they do. These feelings will pass and comfort will return if you're able to keep in mind that every single person you know and meet has at least one skeleton in their own closet.

Now is the time to talk about what will make you happy. You may want to establish a marriage contract with specific details, rules and regulations. This is what a couple in Washington State recently did. They had rules and regulations for 59 situations and expected behaviors. Seems a little rigid but, if it works for them, that's great.

The point is, you alone, or, ideally, you and your spouse, determine what you want out of the relationship. You decide on positive interactions, daily living styles, and a means to solve problems.

Set up a flexible relationship blueprint, a plan that can be altered by talking together. Using the past to understand and construct a positive future gives you the tools to engineer a livable, wonderful life together.

CHAPTER NINE

RECREATING YOUR SELF: SUCCESS THROUGH SEPARATION OR DIVORCE

Making Transitions

You've decided it's time for physical and emotional relief. It's time to divorce. The affair is history, and by taking charge you're changing an intolerable situation. Divorce is action. Divorce is physical relief. You no longer have to be with, or have in your environment, the person causing you pain. Divorce is emotional healing. It finalizes the status of the relationship and resolves turmoil. Divorce is a positive solution, the climax of one portion of life, the opportunity to formulate a new dream and plan a new future.

Divorce is a transition. It's the end of one stage of your adult development and the beginning of another. Sometimes the thought of divorce is frightening and is exacerbated by horror stories people tell about their own experiences or about the horrendous nightmare of a friend's divorce. Face it, there are some bad divorces. Divorce is a transition where nothing is in place. Though relationships, finances, the future and the divorce settlement are unknown, divorce doesn't have to be a nightmare. Knowledge is power. Just like beginning college or beginning a new job, there are preparatory steps necessary to ensure a successful transition.

In this chapter I'll show you how to keep a divorce and your spouse's affair in perspective while you:

- Manage your emotions.
- Make sure your children are physically and psychologically safe.
- See to your financial security.
- Understand the legal system.
- Handle social issues.
- Develop general and specific goals for the future.

If you are the divorce decision-maker, task number one is to make sure you're done with the marriage. Unless you are in a physically abusive situation, it is critical that you avoid doing anything precipitously, as Ann did. Ann was so hurt and angry with her husband, Randy, that she impulsively began a divorce action.

Ann and Randy
Randy, 31, had an affair which was over, but the marriage was shaky. Randy declared, "I'm just not happy with Ann". In fact, he wasn't sure if he ever loved her, and told her they might have to separate to give him time to clear his head.

Ann, 30, was doing everything she could think of to make Randy happy. Still, Randy needed nights out to "have a cigar and chat with the guys," but who "the guys" were remained a mystery.

Ann finally accused Randy of continuing the affair. Randy denied the affair right down to Ann's confrontation of him and his girl friend kissing in Ann's car. Ann did a lot of screaming at the time and mental trashing after the fact: Trashing herself, then trashing Randy.

Ann couldn't justify her behavior and get over her "stupidity" for going along with Randy's cigar routine. She felt hatred and disgust for him and wanted a divorce.

At the same time, she was filled with fear. She anticipated social embarrassment and ostracism by friends who were still couples. She viewed herself as a failure. She was convinced that both sets of parents would be hurt and that her children's futures and emotional well-being would be seriously compromised.

Most of all, Ann said she couldn't stop loving Randy. Nevertheless, she went forward with a divorce action.

Taking Precipitous Action

Ann's decision to divorce was a reaction to Randy's affair and the mistaken idea that her emotional trauma would disappear once she took action. Randy had her jumping through hoops trying to please him; now she would provide a few hoops of her own.

Ann's need to take action was powerful. Jump up, take charge; get rid of the problem and move on. Good! But the idea that removing Randy through divorce would also remove Ann's pain wasn't true. Impulsive decisions fueled by hurt and anger seldom have happy outcomes.

Starting a divorce process without relationship resolution doesn't solve the problem since nothing is understood or worked through. This scenario usually means a divorce is started, stopped, or put on hold--only to be started again at a later date.

Ambivalent and confused, Ann wisely put her divorce on hold. Therapy would settle her down, give her time to think through and verbalize where she is emotionally with Randy, and, if need be, develop an alternate plan. I know a man who started and stopped the divorce process five times!

Deciding to Divorce

You've thought it through. The marriage is over. Either you're not interested in continuing the relationship struggle and feel done with your spouse or the affair has taken your mate over the bridge and out of the marriage.

Of course, if you are the decision-maker, the relationship-leaver, marching ahead has fewer pitfalls than if you are the one being left.

Making the decision to divorce establishes boundaries, settles confusion, you feel as if you are finally moving on with your life. As the leaver, the thought of divorce is painful, yet a relief and a solution. You may love your spouse, but you are not interested in spending next week with this person, let alone the rest of your life. You just want to be rid of your spouse, get that person out of your life.

If, on the other hand, you are being abandoned, making the decision to divorce will be another churning, heart-wrenching, life adjustment. After the betrayal trauma you've been through, it doesn't seem fair that you have to begin another circle of difficulty.

Now, your spouse is your enemy. Because of your spouse you are suffering, angry and without control of your life. You are sailing in uncharted waters.

When you're feeling miserable, in relationship pain and emotionally deadlocked, and when you've explored every other possibility to solve marital problems, divorce can be the best possible solution. Separation means taking charge, putting yourself on the path of growth and development.

Once you've made the monumental decision to divorce, your next hurdle is the divorce process. There is no training course for divorce. It is on-the-job learning. Wending your way through legal proceedings can produce more heartache and long-term bad feelings. However, with knowledge of the legal system, as well as patience and tenacity, you can make your way through the process successfully.

In some situations the divorce begins while you are tying up emotional connections. This was Cheryl's dilemma.

Cheryl and Kevin

A beautiful couple, small, dark, shapely 31-year-old Cheryl, and tall, dark, handsome 30-year-old Kevin, had been married six years. Their attractive façade hid an ugly inner life.

Friends told her, family told her, and she talked to herself about her husband, Kevin's, behavior. Cheryl was angry and said she hated him but also loved his "good side."

Kevin made fun of her in front of others, was sarcastic and mean-spirited when they were alone, and verbally fought with her father and sister. Though both worked full time and Cheryl made more than Kevin, Kevin managed and withheld money.

At the slightest provocation, he raised his voice in anger and made threatening physical gestures. Occasionally he grabbed and slapped Cheryl.

After any altercation Kevin punished Cheryl with silence. Cheryl couldn't stand the tension and made up by writing apologetic notes to him telling him how much she loved him. She would kiss, caress and cajole Kevin into a smile. In other words, Cheryl did everything she could to keep peace between herself and her husband.

Cheryl habituated her mind to ignoring

Kevin's behavior or words that hurt her. Peace at any price was her credo.

When Cheryl discovered an intimate message to Kevin on their answering machine from another woman, she decided she had enough and filed for divorce.

Though everyone encouraged her separation and applauded her decision, Cheryl had what she termed a "nervous breakdown." She cried all the time. Tears streamed down her face at work. She knew a divorce was the right thing to do. She said, "I can't live like this the rest of my life," and she developed a plan to stabilize her moods.

To calm herself and take control, Cheryl consciously put in her mind Kevin's infidelity and nastiness. Otherwise, she began to feel sentimental and think she should soothe him.

As Cheryl stabilized she realized she had to leave her abusive situation. Still, she feared Kevin's anger and knew leaving would be met with rage. Kevin would be a wild man and cause such havoc that an orderly move would be impossible and she knew, if she left without taking her things, he would trash everything.

Cheryl proceeded to plot and plan her escape when Kevin wasn't home. Kevin left for work one morning; Cheryl was packed and gone in the afternoon.

Kevin was shocked by Cheryl's independence. Now he desperately wanted Cheryl. He called. He left notes on her car. He showed up at her beautician's.

Cheryl, in the meantime, began to have a few hours of peace and gradually a day or two of calm. Kevin's desire for her soothed and comforted her. Her self-esteem rose and she began to laugh at Kevin's efforts.

Still, fearful that Kevin would somehow get back at her through the divorce, and though she had an attorney, Cheryl submerged herself in researching divorce laws and the step-by-step divorce process until she felt knowledgeable and had some measure of comfort knowing what to expect. (Whether a divorce is progressing peacefully or grinding painfully, knowledge of the process is smart, helpful and calming.)

By the time the divorce was granted, Cheryl had melancholy moments but overall felt happy with her decision to leave her abusive situation.

Divorce Plan

Whether you are leaving or being left, winding through separation with the least amount of disturbance means thinking through the physical, emotional and social changes that are coming and plotting out what to expect and how you plan to handle the affair issue.

Developing Your Plan

You would not build a house or have a formal church wedding without a detailed blueprint. The same is true of separation. Divorce is uncharted territory, so you need information to understand the divorce process as best you can.

The following information is a general divorce guide focused on affair issues. I also recommend you pick up books which detail each step of the divorce process. Study them, ask questions of your attorney and friends who have divorced, and attend divorce seminars.

The affair is an important part of the decision to divorce; consequently, what you do with affair information is important. Are you going to make the affair central to the divorce, or is it history? If you decide to protect your children from the affair, or avoid embarrassment and scandal for yourself and spouse, you won't suggest, insinuate or give out bits of affair information. You won't broadcast affair information to whomever will listen to prove you are right, to vent hostility, and to make sure your mate doesn't get off scott free.

If you wish to use affair information to influence child custody and division of assets, then it is essential you keep affair details quiet. The satisfaction of telling and being the innocent party pales when you allow your spouse to plan his or her defense and denials.

Carefully think through what outcome is best for you and your children. You want to make a conscious decision, not blurt out or be emotionally driven to verbalize information. Affair information should be kept between you and your attorney.

Predicting the Consequences

When you've been deceived, proceeding to rational thoughts and an evenly balanced emotional state is not simple. Even the fear of losing your back-up person, the sharer of responsibility, as minimal as those efforts seem now, can be frightening to deal with on your own. I'm not saying this to scare you, but to let you know these feelings and thoughts are normal. Most people planning divorce have these concerns.

Divorce is an emotional stressor and the actual process lasts so long (in the majority of cases at least one to two years) that preparing yourself with concrete information about the process and knowing what to expect throughout the proceedings will prove helpful and smooth the legal, emotional path.

To develop your plan examine seven major areas:

1. Handling emotions and remaining stable
2. Communicating during the divorce
3. Caring for children
4. Evaluating environment and financial considerations
5. Understanding the legal system
6. Preparing for social changes
7. Anticipating the future

1. Handling Emotions and Remaining Stable

Divorce means adapting to the unknown, handing your fate over to strangers, and stepping into an unknown world. The idea of divorce, separating from a painful relationship and taking action, is appealing. On the other hand, the possible pitfalls of the legal system are unappealing and frightening, particularly since your recent life was steeped in the unknown with deception and secrets.

Although affair deception is over, your emotions wobble and your thinking lacks clarity. You debate and confuse yourself, "Am I doing the right thing? Why am I getting divorced? Maybe I should stick it out. Maybe I should beg my mate to stay."

If your relationship was excellent before the affair and your spouse immediately took responsibility for his behavior when you discovered the affair, questioning your decision is healthy.

When you question yourself, use the following

checklist that includes the behavior, emotions and communication styles of your spouse that absolutely should not be tolerated.

- Continuing an affair or being involved in repeated adultery.
- Arousing affair suspicions by always being late or not showing up at expected times.
- Following you from room to room and being accusatory; you are responsible and to blame, the affair was your fault.
- Suggesting you may be having an affair, and that's why s/he had an affair.
- Demanding sex, and/or saying sexual incompatibility or lack of sex was the reason for the affair.
- Threatening to make the divorce horrendous or warning that you are in serious trouble if you attempt to leave or mention the affair.
- Lying or changing reality from day to day.

These issues are unacceptable. They are forms of disrespect and, in some cases, abuse.

If you feel indecisive, check the list. If you aren't sure whether your spouse's specific behavior and talk is "normal," check the list. If your spouse accuses you of being overly sensitive and confused or interpreting situations and communication incorrectly, check the list.

2. Communicating During a Divorce

Divorce often brings out the worst in people, particularly when you live in the same house during legal proceedings. Your former mate is now your legal adversary.

Consequently, new guidelines for living together will help you stay calm, regardless of your partner's behavior.

Both dialogue rehearsal and visual rehearsal of potential interactions are helpful when you strive for peace. You know what to expect from your spouse; use that information to your advantage. Don't jump into old behavior and dialogue though you are sorely tempted to "explain" or to "set her/him straight." Rationally discussing the affair is not going to happen. Don't even try.

In general, avoid discussions and debates. In particular, avoid affair topics. They go nowhere and solve nothing.

Basic communication guidelines include:

- Don't talk about the affair.
- Be polite; act as though your spouse is a co-worker.
- Avoid all conflict or arguments (just walk away).
- Don't discuss property settlement.
- Don't talk about child custody.
- Do take any statements your spouse makes with a grain of salt. In other words, doubt the veracity of any divorce related statements.
- Don't give any information to your spouse; you may unwittingly jeopardize your divorce case.
- Expect your spouse to try to undermine your attorney.
- Don't agree to anything. Don't sign anything or negotiate with your spouse without your attorney.

It is difficult to live in a house together and not share some information. The urge to talk is powerful. Keep your contact to small talk about the weather, logistics with the kids, or specific household items.

3. Caring for Children

As soon as you are positive divorce is imminent, let your children know. Do not mention the divorce in casual conversation or suggest it may happen; getting a divorce is not casual conversation.

You're the adult. Keep your words simple and straightforward, avoid histrionics and do not mention the affair.

If it's possible for you and your husband to cooperate, you need to sit down together and let the children know you are getting divorced, that your love for them is unchanged, you are not divorcing them and you will both remain active, loving parents.

Keep reminding yourself this is not the time to fight or get back at the other person. You are giving your children important information about their lives and what to expect. Inform them of any changes in their environment. Do not promise anything at this time about future living arrangements, and don't encourage them to take sides or make any decisions about who they are going to live with. Overtly or covertly blaming your spouse isn't helpful to your children.

Pointing the finger and criticizing with the idea that they will feel sorry for you and mad at your spouse turns you into the child.

You might say, "Don't they have a right to know what's going on?" Not necessarily, since children do not understand the world or relationships as adults do. They interpret your words from a child's mind.

As adults, we can barely manage our thinking and emotions in affair crisis and divorce fear. Save divorce blame and acrimony talk for your therapist.

Let your children talk, cry or even be silent. They

may have expected your divorce; they may be relieved or they may be stunned. Encourage further talks.

Buy divorce books appropriate for their ages and get some books for yourself on parenting, divorce, emotions, successful separating, whatever. Books can be soothing as well as informational.

Seek Counseling

If you have any concern that your child is experiencing difficulty with your marital situation, call a child psychologist and make an appointment for an evaluation. Child psychologists are trained to help children work through emotional turmoil resulting from family chaos or any other childhood problem.

Older children usually don't want to go, and will often state that, if you force them to go, they won't talk. They say they are just fine. Nevertheless, if you are worried, make the appointment. Counselors are trained to talk to children who won't talk. And believe me, children talk. Usually they talk their heads off.

You may also worry that taking children for counseling sends a message that something's emotionally or mentally wrong with them. As a rule, that's a concern of the parents. It's your thought, not your child's.

Children are magical thinkers and take on responsibility for a parent's pain. Children may never verbalize what they think or feel because their thinking is concrete. They don't have words to describe their feelings, and/or don't want to hurt you. They think their understanding of the situation is correct.

So, present the counseling appointment to your child as your issue. You are worried. You are concerned that your divorce action is causing problems for your children and you want to make sure they are O.K. Explain that you would not let them walk around with a physical problem without seeing a doctor, and you believe that their mental functioning and emotional life are as important as any other part of them.

Involving the Children Emotionally

The idea that maintaining the family is critical regardless of the circumstances is unrealistic. Life is not perfect and children are not aided in their growth and development by cold, angry or fighting parents who stay together "for the sake of the children."

Your intense, emotional struggle through this separation and divorce probably leaves little energy for your children. Certainly not the energy you normally had for play and interactions. Guilt crops up. Guilt can be helpful since it brings your focus back to parenting. When you have a guilt attack, use it to help yourself by attending to your children's needs.

Remember, it is inappropriate to use your children as therapists--crying, complaining and revealing private information about the affair. Children are not mature enough to understand the complexities of the problems, nor should they be put in the middle as arbitrators or pitted against the other parent. If there are times when you slip into this behavior, stop it the second you hear yourself. Give your mind advance notice that you will cease and desist discussing all but global issues with your children.

Global issues are, "Yes, we are getting divorced. I don't know the exact date." If you are crying or emotional, say, "I am having a bad day because of the divorce," and follow that up with your feelings: You feel angry, hurt, sad.

These expressions help your children empathize with you, and serve as a model for their own feelings. Your verbalization of feelings help them understand feelings can be talked about and safely expressed.

Feelings are a part of us. By putting words to your feelings, your children learn that a person can have powerful feelings, but that feelings don't have to be acted out or projected onto someone else. (An example of projection: "*You make* me angry." No. Anger is my feeling, not yours. I am reacting to you. Rather than projecting, ideally you take responsibility and say, "When you do that, I feel angry.")

It's important to verbalize to your children that having feelings and expressing them is not wrong or stupid, Rather, such expression of feeling is natural and important. Your words and actions show your children how you feel. Then they can apply your words and expressions to their own feelings and use your emotional behavior as a model for handling their feelings.

4. Evaluating Environmental and Financial Considerations

As I indicated in earlier chapters, be smart about assets. Don't let emotions cloud the reality of finances. **Protect yourself immediately.**

Securing Your Assets

Secure and document every single asset, including sentimental, seemingly insignificant items, and every debt, including who owes what. Once marital assets are gone, you're out of luck.

Men usually feel the home is theirs, the children are theirs and any assets are theirs. They are more apt to begin an immediate campaign psychologically ("I make the money" or "I've made the most money, so this is all mine"). Men are also more apt to secrete cash, stocks, bonds, business items, anything.

Women are shocked by this view and behavior, but

the truth is, the person who immediately takes charge of finances has the advantage.

Securing Your Home

Impulsiveness in a divorce works against you. For example, Joanne couldn't stand the fractious environment she lived in with Stan. They fought over a look, a word, and, in particular, over her affair.

Against her attorney's advice, Joanne left and moved in with her married daughter. Two years later the house is still on the market. Stan is happy as a clam to be in the home. So far he has been able to sabotage every potential sale. Joanne is still miserable, plus she's filled with rage at Stan's failure to sell the house.

Advice: Do not make any quick moves

If you have a choice, do not make any quick moves. At the same time, be prepared for the sale of real estate. Being drop-kicked out of your home because of an affair is beyond changing environments; it's trauma. On one hand, you no longer want your home because there are so many bad memories attached and the comfort of home is gone. On the other hand, you didn't make the choice, you've been forced out or you fear the new person will inhabit your home and that horrifies you.

Remember, you live inside yourself. Your inner view colors and frames wherever you are. Home isn't mortar and brick. Home is where the heart is, where security and, hopefully, peace are found. People all want to go home!

So, Goodbye! That was one phase of life. Now you are on to new, happy experiences. Wherever you decide to go, you will be able to turn that house into home.

Deciding How to Divide Assets

Two households do not live as cheaply as one. That's a fact. If you haven't already done so, take paper and pen and plot out the best and worst possible financial scenario. Determine your needs, then your attorney will tell you what is financially in your best interest and what is possible.

If your divorce goes to mediation or trial, the affair may be a factor that will give you an advantage, depending upon evidence, the mediator's point of view, your lawyer's skill and the judge's prejudices.

5. Understanding the Legal System

The divorce may be your first encounter with a lawyer and the legal system. Stepping into the unknown is frightening, particularly because of emotional turmoil and because it feels like your life is out of control. Force yourself to stay calm and focus on what you want from the divorce.

Your attorney is your employee and works for you. Be honest about what you've been through, but realize your attorney will dramatize your plight when the complaint is filed. So if you prefer a low key divorce without blame, immediately indicate that you need to look over the complaint before your spouse is served.

You need an attorney who is a family divorce specialist, knows what to expect from each judge, and is a person you feel confident can stand up to and, if need be, best your spouse's attorney. Personally, you want to feel rapport and support. You want to know your attorney is in your corner and will fight for you every step of the way.

Ask your attorney for step-by-step progress reports on filings, time frames, and when input will be needed from you. When will the attorney get in touch with you and how do you reach her or him. This seems simple, it seldom is. Attorneys often are busy and may take several days to return calls. Weeks between conversations will elevate your anxiety.

Find out how you make immediate contact should you have an emergency. If you can, pin down communication expectations. Ask your attorney what the charges per hour or per case will be. Also ask about additional costs if there are complications such as motions or petitions.

Beginning the Divorce Process

If your attorney files a Complaint for Divorce first, you are the plaintiff. The Complaint and a Summons will then be served upon your husband/wife, the defendant.

When the Complaint is served, your spouse will no doubt be upset and angry because the Complaint is exactly what it says: You are complaining in order to get a divorce. Though many states have no-fault divorces, your Complaint indicates a problem. Your spouse's lawyer then has a certain number of days to reply, depending on the state in which you live.

Discussing the Divorce Is Not Wise

Unless you and your spouse are in complete, friendly agreement about the divorce, discussing any aspect of the divorce isn't helpful. Don't suggest that you have an ace up your sleeve about the affair. You may or may not have an advantage because of the affair. Don't give out information that you don't want your spouse to have or get into a disagreement that is pointless. As difficult as it is, try to maintain a friendly but uninformative stance.

Be discrete when you talk about personal issues and legal proceedings with relatives and friends. Forget blaming or focusing on the affair. It's almost impossible to be totally silent about the divorce. In fact, you do need a confidante. However, to tell the world about your private life is unwise.

Answering nosy questions isn't necessary. Others will be very interested in the details of your relationship and divorce, but just because they ask doesn't mean you have to answer. Simply indicate the subject is too painful to talk about.

Staying Calm During the Case

By the middle of your divorce you will begin to feel fidgety and anxious to get it over with. Stay calm. Divorces wear everyone down.

Be prepared for court cancellations and for your attorney and your spouse's attorney to be unavailable for scheduled appearances. Realize that your expectations for divorce completion may be off by at least six months to a year. Some divorces last two or three years. You're in for the long haul, so settle down.

Bonnie and Dick

Bonnie, 45, a popular clothes store manager with three children, called for counseling while she and her husband, Dick, 43, an auto company executive, were in the process of divorce.

Bonnie began, "Everyone thinks we're crazy because we're having a pleasant divorce. Friends say our attitude won't last. They remember last year.

"The year before we started the divorce was terrible. I was out of my mind about Dick's affair. We were nasty with one another, and we drew anyone who would listen into our conflict.

"Each of us felt righteous (although I never did understand why Dick didn't just say he was sorry), and that this situation had developed with good reason. Of course, most family members and friends wanted to be helpful. They put in their two cents worth and took sides.

"Well, they're dumbfounded now. Our kids are settling down. We just quit quarreling. I got sick of hearing myself go on and on about his affair, plus, the emotional turmoil was making me sick. Finally, I just felt done. Like I had roasted long enough, burnt off all my rage and wanted to move on. I can't tell you what a relief that day was for me.

"So, you're probably wondering why I called you for counseling, since I sound like I feel so sure of myself. Frankly, I worry that this state is temporary and suddenly an emotional backlash will begin. I think I need someone objective to talk to."

Aiming for a Healthy Divorce

Bonnie is smart. She's right. She needs an objective view of herself and her relationship. And she may need assistance to carry off a "positive" divorce. She's already seen that when she and her husband calmed themselves and used their heads, both they and their children benefited.

Stability can also be provided by a psychologist. Divorce is second on the list of life stressors, and a therapist's objective view helps you eliminate confusion and provides emotional support.

A positive divorce seems like an oxymoron. We generally view divorce in negative terms: as failure, disassociation of a partnership, disappointment and dissolution of the family. Most people aren't able to turn themselves around and eliminate confusion the way Bonnie and Dick did, but it can be done.

Getting through the process with a pragmatic, no-nonsense approach means having information about the process and an intellectual plan to handle emotional issues.

If you know up front that staying with the plan may be difficult, you can develop methods to get through the ragged, nasty emotional stretches.

Achieving Finality

The end of this grueling experience can heat up as you tie up all the loose ends and make final decisions. Rushing to finalize the divorce is not smart.

Disposition of all joint items is a must at the end of the divorce. You don't want long, dragged-out, post-divorce legal problems because financial and custody issues weren't nailed down.

Make sure you complete custody and property settlements. Cover all your bases.

6. Preparing for Social Changes

Although your social group will shift and grow, and friends and acquaintances will adapt to your different role, feeling comfortable and normal in social settings takes time. An opening conversational gambit is often the "why" of your divorce. Placing blame on your spouse with affair exploits is not a class act. Although it is tempting, avoid talk about the affair.

If you feel shy or out of place because you're in the divorce process, get into a divorce group for support. Visit the library or book store and stock up on books about transitions into single life. Look for groups who will help you deal with a spouse's affair. You don't have to reinvent the wheel; many people have gone before you and can tell you exactly what to expect and how to make the transition successfully.

It's up to you to keep in contact with friends. Feeling sad, awkward or out of place when you're with couple friends is normal. It will change.

Preparing for the Future
Finding the Right Partner

Affairs and divorces turn people into relationship skeptics. You're fearful of being hurt again or, spousal loss results in a desperate need for a person, any person. Your defenses rush in to protect your psyche. You develop a smothering need to be close or, a fearful stance and need to be distant. The truth is, people remain the same, some are trustworthy, some are not.

Unfortunately, you have been burned. Your naiveté is gone and you now know just how much pain can be inflicted by the one you love.

Individuals are afraid of their own judgments after their partner's affair. In retrospect, you believe you showed poor judgment in choosing a love object who would hurt you so badly, so why would you trust yourself to choose wisely now?

Living is learning. It's like being in school. When you've made a huge error and it's brought to your attention, the correction is riveted in your mind.

As a marriage counselor and relationship expert I'm often asked, how do you know if a new person is the right person? What criteria do you use?

Relax and focus on the here and now. View every new person as interesting friend material, just as you would if you were getting to know a same sex individual. Like a psychologist, delve into what his or her life was like before you met. Use empathy and listening skills while simultaneously paying attention to your own reactions to tone, facial expressions, and ability to connect with you.

Practice making a friend of everyone you meet, male or female. Eliminate the stress that comes with potential courting. If h/she turns out to be an acquaintance, good. A friend? Even better.

The rest of your life will not be determined by the affair crisis you have lived through

Affairs happen. The searing pain will disappear. With your present knowledge you are alerted to secrets and betrayal; your antennae are up and you will catch the slightest hint of deceit.

In the future if you sense, intuit or have evidence of any misconduct on the part of a new friend, investigate immediately. If you sense a problem, don't tuck away your partner's feeble or seemingly reality-oriented explanation.

I understand you don't want to be paranoid or on the investigative prowl endlessly, but when you feel suspicious get to the bottom of it immediately.

Depersonalize and recognize that affairs are the expression of the person having the affair

Look without, not within, when another person's behavior is unacceptable. In other words, hold yourself responsible for your behavior; other people, not you, are responsible for their behavior.

This is true for any behavior, although we often feel compelled to react. You choose to react, just as you decide to act. No one makes you do it.

A new person you're with or are interested in is not basing talk and actions on you, although we can guess that person wants to please. Action, thoughts and emotion are

Success: Separation Or Divorce

generated from the other person's mind, and that's where you want to keep them; in the other person's mind, not yours. Don't personalize. Their talk isn't relevant to you except to give you information about them. If you feel uncomfortable with words or behavior, take your experience seriously and discuss your feelings or remove yourself.

Your next romantic liaison will begin with like, as in friendship, and evolve into love

The critical element in a successful relationship is friendship. You want your lover also to be your best friend, a person you respect and trust. Wanting a companion and desiring a love relationship are healthy desires. The unhealthy end of the spectrum is desperately needing a mate to feel happy, fulfilled and worthwhile. Desperation puts you in jeopardy of choosing an unsuitable, undesirable person.

You already know what it's like to be in a troubled coupling. If your thoughts continually turn to the need for an immediate partner, your thoughts are irrational. Your total existence is not defined by love.

Annette and Brad

Annette, a 27-year-old accountant, found her 29-year-old husband Brad, a race car driver, in their bed, in their bedroom, with her friend, Diane.

Annette went crazy for a week, was hysterical for another two weeks. Then she went into a deep depression for four weeks. Finally, when she came out of her depression, she forgave Brad and wanted him back. He said, "No way," blamed Annette for his affair and began a divorce action.

Brad said, "You know I've always loved only you, but you were such a bitch about the Diane situation, there's no way I can live with that. Diane means nothing to me."

This statement came immediately before Brad divorced Annette and he married Diane.

Brad's marriage didn't deter Annette's pursuit of Brad. She phoned him daily at home and at work, declaring her love and her sorrow for not understanding his feelings. She suggested sex and tried to make luncheon or dinner dates. She showed up in his work parking lot.

Finally, Diane, not Brad, told Annette to knock it off or a PPO (Personal Protection Order) would be issued requiring Annette either stay away from Brad or be jailed.

Surviving Without Your Spouse

It's hard to feel compassion for Annette or Brad. Both lack character. Annette's obsessive behavior is not uncommon. Many people want their spouse back despite an affair. Annette's desire was about fear and loneliness. Relationship misery didn't matter; Annette couldn't survive without a mate.

You know the end of the story. When she finally got it that Brad was never coming back, Annette's obsession shifted to a co-worker. He's available to her for the moment and she's happy--for now.

Knowing a person well and taking time to develop friendship lays the groundwork for and the possibility of an intimate, satisfactory, long-term connection. Need obliterates knowing.

Develop Agreements Based On Trust

Spell out what you expect from a partner. For example, you may be uncomfortable with former lover/spouse contact; opposite sex luncheons; sins of omission, such as secret phone calls; flirting or excessive dances with another person (excessive may be two, depending upon your definition).

If you both understand the rules, you won't live in a gray area. Either behavior is within acceptable boundaries or it isn't. Honesty is critical for trust and intimacy. When you discover your lover's understanding of the rules is different than yours, clear it up as quickly as possible and don't argue about who's right.

Find a therapist if either you or your chosen person is so jealous that glancing at another is taken as flirting. See a therapist when you want to talk to your partner about behavior that seems inappropriate to you though your partner says you are reading it incorrectly.

Both your behavior and your partner's spell trouble in such cases.

Learning to Question If Something Sounds Wrong

As human beings we tend to interpret another person's words and action from our own experience and point of view. This is natural and necessary--how else can it be interpreted?

If you notice yourself puzzling over words or behavior, check it out. Ask questions. Do not let perplexing issues pass by, no matter how difficult or even embarrassing it is to zero in for answers.

Generally, people are happy to talk about themselves, explain their point of view or why they acted in a particular way. The way you inquire will affect the response you get. If your tone implies criticism, is curt or sharp, expect the same in reply. If you are truly interested in information, that too will be apparent.

View yourself as a truth-seeker. People are good at putting up fronts and presenting what they think is acceptable or appealing to others.

Your task is to get beyond the mask, if there is one, to what is real. That's why rushing to commitment can be a huge mistake. Patience will tell you what's real; time is your ally.

Anticipating the Future

You've been through two major life stressors and you've successfully landed on your feet. Since life is a series of small and large problems, your skill in marching through the emotional and situational turmoil you've endured is a guide for future challenges. You tackled divorce and affair issues, you developed goals and plans to facilitate the goals and took action.

You are a work in progress, growing and changing. You are on an upward trajectory. **The affair is over; it's history. The divorce is over. You are free.**

CHAPTER TEN

Bittersweet

Now you've read *Affairs: Emergency Tactics*. Here's how I imagine you've successfully handled your partner's affair.

Every step you took was important. You began by establishing evidence that an affair was in progress. Next, you decided what to do with the evidence and you found that you were not the helpless victim, no matter how badly your partner behaved. Your actions were consequential. Had you acted impulsively and foolishly, the outcome would have been disastrous.

At first, you were on an emotional roller coaster. Monster depressions clouded every day, blotting out the occasional hopeful, positive thought. Then, slowly, the roller coaster of emotions turned into feeling waves which periodically grabbed and stabbed you. Finally peace of mind arrived, not all the time, but often enough that you knew you'd survive the ordeal.

Once you analyzed the type of affair your partner was involved in, you were able to focus your resources more effectively. It hurt like hell, but you knew what to do. If it was a bridge out of the relationship arrangement, you learned to give up the struggle and say, "Good-bye"--with dignity. If it was self-serving, you knew that you were faced with repetitive assaults on your dignity and life style. If the affair was meant to repair your relationship, you were able to put it in perspective and save your marriage.

Recognizing affair categories provided you with solutions. You struggled with the information. If the affair was self-serving or a bridge out, you knew you were on the path to separation. On the other hand, the repair affair revealed options for the partnership: status quo, separation or a healthier, happier marriage.

You've lived through a major emotional trauma and you've done it well. Getting through an affair is one of the most difficult things you will do in your life. Sifting through the tumult, picking up the pieces, and making decisions for yourself about your life has been frightening but also enlightening and empowering. You know now that you can prevail under very difficult circumstances.

Affairs turn sweet people bitter, but not you. You are alive, you are well, you lived through it when you often thought you wouldn't. New opportunities have opened up to you that you could not imagine in the depths of your despair. You're on your way to an even better life.

BIBLIOGRAPHY

Avery, Caryl S. 1989. How do you build intimacy in an age of divorce. *Psychology Today*, May: 27-31.
Beck, Aaron T. 1988. *Love is never enough.* New York: Harper & Row.
Bergman, Stephen J., & Surrey, J. 1992. The woman-man relationship: Impasses and possibilities. *Work in Progress*, No. 55. Wellesley, MA: Stone Center Working Papers Series.
Bernard, J. 1972. *The future of marriage.* New York: World.
Botwin, Carol. 1988. *Men who can't be faithful.* New York: Warner Books.
Branden, Nathaniel. 1992. *The power of self-esteem.* Deerfield Beach, FL: Health Communications.
Brown, Emily M. 1993. The open secret. *Family Therapy Networker,* May/June: 39-45
Brown, Emily M. 1991. *Patterns of infidelity and their treatment.* New York: Brunner Mazel.
Brown, Laura S. and Root, Maria. (Eds.)1990. *Diversity and complexity in feminist therapy.* New York: Harrington Park Press.
Burns, David D. 1990. *The feeling good handbook.* New York: Penguin Books.
Coopersmith, Stanley. 1967. *The antecedents of self-esteem.* San Francisco: W. H. Freeman.
Cramer, Kathryn D. 1990. *Staying on top when your world turns upside down.* New York: Penguin Books.
Engel, Beverly. 1990. *The emotionally abused woman.* New York: Ballantine.
Ericsson, Stephanie.1992. The ways we lie, *Utne Reader,* Nov/Dec: 56-58.
Fisher, Helen E. 1992. Anatomy of love. New York:

W. W. Norton & Co.

Friday, Nancy. 1980. *Men in love.* New York: Dell Publishing.

Forward, Susan, & Craig Buck. 1991. *Obsessive love.* New York: Bantam Books.

Gaylin, Willard, & Person, Ethel. (Eds.) 1988. *Passionate attachments: Thinking about love.* New York: The Free Press.

Goldberg, Herb. 1983. *The new male/female relationship.* New York: Signet.

Gray, Paul. 1993. What is love? *Time,* February 15:47-49.

Heyn, Dalma. 1992. *The erotic silence of the American wife.* New York: Random House.

Hendrick, Susan, & Hendrick, Clyde. 1992. *Liking, loving and relating.* Pacific Grove, CA: Brooks/Cole Publishing Co.

Hendrix, Harville. 1988. *Getting the love you want: A guide for couples.* New York: Harper & Row.

Interview with Angelou Mayou. 1993. *USA Weekend,* Oct. 8: 4-7.

Jacobson, Neil S. & Gurman, Alan S. 1995. *Clinical handbook of couple therapy.* New York: Guilford Press.

James, W. 1980. *Principles of psychology.* 2 Vols. New York: Holt.

Jordan, Judith V. 1992. Relational resilience. *Work in Progress,* No. 57. Wellesley, MA: Stone Center Working Paper Series.

Landers, Ann. 1993. From head over heals stuff. *The Detroit News and Free Press,* Sunday, February 14: 2L.

Lawson, Annette. 1988. *Adultery: An analysis of love and betrayal.* New York: Basic Books.

Lerner, Harriet Goldher. 1985. *The dance of anger.* New York: Harper & Row.

Livermore, Beth. 1993. The lessons of love,

Psychology Today, March/April: 30-80.
Love, Patricia and Robinson, Jo. 1994. *Hot monogamy.* New York: Penguin Books.
McKay, Matthew and Fanning, Patrick. 1992. *Self Esteem.* Oakland, CA.: New Harbinger.
Moultrup, David J. 1990. *Husbands and lovers.* New York: Guilford Press.
Murstein, Bernard. (Ed.) 1978. *Exploring intimate life styles.* New York: Springer.
Norwood, Robin.1985.*Women who love too much.* New York: Pocket Books, Simon & Schuster, Inc.
Notarius, Clifford and Markman, Howard. 1994. Six truths for couples, *Psychology Today,* Jan/Feb: 24-25.
Oldham, John M. and Morris, Lois B. 1995.*New personality self-portrait.* New York: Bantam Books.
Paglia, Camille. 1993. It's a jungle out there, so get used to it! *Utne Reader,* Jan/Feb: 61-65.
Pittman, Frank. 1989. *Private lies.* New York: W. W. Norton.
Rich, Adrienne. 1979. *On lies, secrets, and silence:* Selected Prose: 1966-1978. New York: W. W. Norton & Co.
Rhodes, Carol L. and Goldner, Norman G. 1993. *Why women & men don't get along.* Troy, MI: Somerset Publishing.
Roberts, Thomas W. 1992. Sexual attraction and romantic love: Forgotten variables in marital therapy. *Journal of Marital and Family Therapy,*18, (4) 357-364.
Schneider, Jennifer P. 1992. *Back from betrayal.* New York: Ballantine Books.
Secunda, Victoria. 1992. Women and their fathers. New York: Delta.
Shapiro, David. 1965. *Neurotic styles.* New York: Basic

Books, Inc.
Shearer, Marguerite & Marshall. 1992. Ladder of love has 7 rungs for a aspirants who seek the heights. *Detroit Free Press*, April 5: 2F.
Steinem, Gloria. 1992. *Revolution from within: A book of self-esteem.* Boston: Little, Brown & Co.
Toufexis, Anastasia. 1993. The right chemistry,*Time*, February 15: 49-51.
Viorst, Judith. 1987. *Unnecessary losses.* New York: Ballantine.
Vaughan, Peggy. 1989. *The monogamy myth.* New York: Newmarket Press.
Weil, Bonnie Eaker and Winter, Ruth. 1993. *Adultery, the forgivable sin.* Secaucus, N. J.: The Carol Publishing Group.
Whitehurst, R. N. 1969. Extramarital sex: Alienation or extension of normal behavior. In G. Neubeck (Ed.), *Extramarital relations,* 93-99. Englewood Cliffs. New Jersey: Prentice-Hall
Wills, T. A. and Weiss, R. L., and Patterson, G. R. 1974. A behavioral analysis of the determinants of marital satisfaction. *Journal of Consulting and Clinical Psychology*, 42, 802-811.
Yorburg, Betty. 1993. *Family relationships.* New York: St. Martin's Press, Inc.